Speaking Up

Speaking Up

Manageable, Meaningful, and Student-Driven Conferences

Anita Abraham and Amy Matthusen

ROWMAN & LITTLEFIELD
Lanham • Boulder • New York • London

Published by Rowman & Littlefield
An imprint of The Rowman & Littlefield Publishing Group, Inc.
4501 Forbes Boulevard, Suite 200, Lanham, Maryland 20706
www.rowman.com

6 Tinworth Street, London SE11 5AL

Copyright © 2021 by Anita Abraham and Amy Matthusen

All rights reserved. No part of this book may be reproduced in any form or by any electronic or mechanical means, including information storage and retrieval systems, without written permission from the publisher, except by a reviewer who may quote passages in a review.

British Library Cataloguing in Publication Information Available

Library of Congress Cataloging-in-Publication Data Available

Names: Abraham, Anita, 1975– author. | Matthusen, Amy, 1974– author.
Title: Speaking up : manageable, meaningful, and student-driven conferences / Anita Abraham and Amy Matthusen.
Description: Lanham : Rowman & Littlefield Publishing, [2021] | Includes bibliographical references. | Summary: "This practical, teacher-friendly text considers strategies for managing the logistics of conferencing with 100+ students, and moving the preparation, and direction of conferences from teacher to student"—Provided by publisher.
Identifiers: LCCN 2021013148 (print) | LCCN 2021013149 (ebook) | ISBN 9781475853704 (cloth) | ISBN 9781475853711 (paperback) | ISBN 9781475853728 (epub)
Subjects: LCSH: Communication in education. | Teacher–student relationships. | Computer conferencing in education. | Teacher effectiveness. | Student-centered learning.
Classification: LCC LB1033.5 .A26 2021 (print) | LCC LB1033.5 (ebook) | DDC 371.102/2—dc23
LC record available at https://lccn.loc.gov/2021013148
LC ebook record available at https://lccn.loc.gov/2021013149

Contents

Foreword   vii
    Carl Anderson
Preface   ix
Acknowledgments   xi
Introduction   xiii
    Christina Ponzio
    Why Writing Conferences?   xiv
    Contextualizing Conferences in the Writing Workshop Model   xv
    Overview of the Book   xvi

Part I: Broader Context and Getting Started   1

1   Building a Culture of Conferencing   3
      Critical Attributes: Qualities of a Strong Classroom Culture   4
      Starting the Year off Right: Building Classroom Culture from the First Day   5
      Keep the Ball Rolling: Nurturing Culture throughout the Year   12
      Pivoting from Culture to Conferencing: Starting the Conversation   18
      Summary   20

2   Getting Organized and Overcoming the Biggest Hurdles   23
      What Materials Do I Need to Get Started?   24
      How Do I Organize the Classroom?   28
      How Do I Structure Class Time?   29
      What Should a Conference Look Like?   30
      How Do I Train the Class to Let Us Talk?   31
      How Do I See Every Student for a Conference?   33
      What Other Resources Can I Use to Conference with More Students?   34
      What Are the Other Students Doing?   36
      How Do I Monitor the Rest of the Class?   39
      How Do I Measure Success When Students Do Not Buy In?   41
      Summary   41

Part II: Tools and Examples for Specific Types of Conferences — 43

3 Before Writing: Brainstorming and Outlining — 45
  Examples and Practices for Brainstorming Conferences — 46
  Examples and Practices for Outlining Conferences — 53
  What Are Other Students Doing? — 57
  Summary — 58

4 During Writing: Drafting Conferences — 59
  Examples and Practices for Drafting Conferences — 60
  What Are Other Students Doing? — 67
  Summary — 67

5 Revision Conferences — 69
  Examples and Practices for Revision Conferences — 70
  Transcript of Audio Comments — 74
  What Are Other Students Doing? — 82
  Summary — 86

6 Reflective and Portfolio Conferences — 89
  Examples and Practices for Reflective Conferences — 90
  What Are Other Students Doing? — 97
  Summary — 98

Part III: Reflection — 101

7 Challenges, Time Constraints, and Next Steps — 103
  Challenge: How Do I See Every Student for a Conference? — 103
  Challenge: Which Classes Should I Conference With? — 104
  Challenge: What Is the Rest of the Class Doing? — 104
  Challenge: How Do I Free Up Class Time? — 104
  Challenge: Other Possible Obstacles to Conferencing — 106
  Challenge: How Do I Address the Issue of Students Who Do Not Want to Conference? — 106
  Challenge: What Are My Next Steps? — 107
  Conclusion — 110

References — 113
About the Authors — 115

Foreword

Carl Anderson

As you read Anita Abraham and Amy Matthusen's *Speaking Up*, keep in mind that conferring was first written about as a methodology professors used with their college students. In the 1960s, Pulitzer Prize–winning author Don Murray, a professor at the University of New Hampshire, wrote a groundbreaking book on teaching writing, *A Writer Teaches Writing*, in which he described the power of having one-on-one writing conferences with his students.

However, despite conferring's roots in college teaching, the common view of conferring among educators is that it's something that elementary school teachers do with their students, not high school teachers. In part, this may be because in 1984 Don Murray's friend and colleague at the University of New Hampshire, Donald Graves, wrote the book *Writing: Teachers and Children at Work*, which became highly influential with elementary school teachers and inspired them to launch writing workshops in their classrooms and start conferring with their students. In the decades since, many educators, such as Lucy Calkins, Ralph Fletcher, Katie Wood Ray, and many others, have written books on teaching writing that have helped many elementary school teachers, in particular, make writing workshops the way they teach writing.

Anita and Amy's book disrupts the idea that conferring with student writers is something that only teachers of our youngest students do. Standing on the shoulders of other educators who have written about teaching writing with secondary students, among them Nancie Atwell, Linda Rief, Tom Romano, Penny Kittle, and Kelly Gallagher, Anita and Amy show us that conferring is indeed possible in high school.

Anita and Amy's book comes out of their own day-to-day experience of conferring with their students. They teach in a secondary school in Flushing, Queens, in New York City, and every day face some of the most difficult challenges that public school teachers around the United States grapple with. They teach more than a hundred students a day, a majority of whom come from families at or below the poverty level. Many of their students are recent immigrants and have come from countries all over the world. Not surprisingly, many of their students are emergent bilinguals. From reading the stories about individual students such as Anthony or Priya that they've included in the book, you'll see that they deal with the wide range of situations high school teachers encounter with their students every day.

The second thing you should know about Anita and Amy is that they have developed their conferring skills over time, through a lot of hard work. They are not superhero teachers who magically started conferring perfectly with students on day one. In fact, they write with incredible honesty about the challenging process they went through to make conferring the heart of the way they teach writing to their students. It takes a lot of courage to begin their book with the sentence, "Our first attempts at conferencing did not go well." By giving us a window into their own growth as writing teachers who confer with their students, they'll give you the permission to embark on your own journey of discovery and learning as you, too, learn to confer.

As you read the book, you will also get hands-on, practical advice about how to make conferring work with your own high school students. Anita and Amy discuss strategies for creating a classroom culture that will make conferring comfortable for adolescents. They have plenty to say about the nuts-and-bolts work of how to schedule conferences in classrooms full of students with varied needs. And they'll help you envision a wide range of conferences that you can have to support students at every stage of the writing process, from brainstorming ideas to drafting and revising their pieces. In sum, this is a comprehensive book about conferring in which Anita and Amy give you answers to the most important questions about conferring with high school writers.

The final and most important thing that you should know about Anita and Amy is that they think of conferring as the most important part of the teaching we do with adolescents in the English classroom. For it's in these conversations with students that we develop the substantial relationships that are essential if they are to learn about writing from us. Developing these relationships isn't the happy by-product of conferring but one of its most important goals. How grateful we should be that Anita and Amy have written a guidebook that shows us how to develop these relationships that will enable students to develop as writers so that they can get their unique and precious voices out into the world.

Carl Anderson,
literacy consultant and author of *How's It Going? A Practical Guide to Conferring with Student Writers* and *A Teacher's Guide to Writing Conferences*

Preface

Our first attempts at conferencing did not go well. We made plenty of mistakes. We didn't prepare properly. Didn't give the kids tools to prepare. We struggled (and still struggle) to create meaningful work for the students outside of conferences. Our pacing was off.

But students continued to tell us how helpful conferencing was. We learned more about our students and understood their struggles inside the classroom and out. We could see that our feedback from these conversations was more meaningful and led to greater strides in students' writing. Students weren't passive recipients of feedback; they were part of a conversation about their own learning.

So we took a deep breath, and decided to give conferencing another try. We made new and different mistakes. We tried to see every student at one point in the writing process: during revisions. With five classes of twenty to thirty students, that's some 125 conversations. We tested the limits of our sanity, giving up lunch periods and running after kids whenever we could capture a few minutes with them. The logistics were overwhelming.

So we took another deep breath, and considered other ways to carve out time to conference and figure out the best practices to make this work. We've found ways to place these conversations at different points of the writing process. We've tested tools to protect classroom time and utilized technology in different ways. We've honed our practices and preparation to make the conversations more meaningful. Keeping time focused and productive is not a puzzle we've fully solved, but we have substantially more tools to bring to bear and help us through the process. With more teaching years under our belts, we have stronger organization and are better at leveraging student buy-in. The following chapters represent the product of a lot of trial and error, and we are always learning.

This work has taken place in our own corner of the world where we teach: a small public high school in Flushing, Queens, in New York City. Our school is a middle/high school with grades 6 through 12, and we are also designated Title I, with the vast majority of families at or below the poverty level. Our students come from all over the world: China, Mexico, Japan, Barbados, Korea, Malaysia, Jamaica, India, Colombia, Paraguay, and the list goes on. Many speak another langauge at home. They have a variety of skill levels speaking, writing, and reading in English, and our courses are planned around these varied proficiencies.

While our own experience draws from over fifteen years of teaching all grades of high school, we are mindful as we write these chapters that our readers come into teaching with a range of backgrounds and student populations. We remember well the challenges of our first years teaching, with seemingly endless work, bumpy classroom management skills, and so many responsibilities beyond just teaching our classes.

For that reason, we have tried to remember the range of contexts in considering our suggestions and explanations for practices. Teachers are at different levels of experience. Many may be teaching middle school rather than high school. Student populations will represent a range of skills, backgrounds, and levels of engagement. We have attempted to be thoughtful in the examples and explanations so that they might be adapted to these different contexts.

As we wrote, we constantly thought, *What would we want out of this book?* Specific, practical, and real examples that would improve our practices and help foster a student-centered classroom. Therefore, for newer teachers, we have tried to lay out examples in detail and provide supplemental materials to replicate for teachers' use. For experienced teachers, we hope that practices and resources will add to their toolboxes.

Our end goal in these practices is to find ways to give up the reins in the classroom. As planners and leaders in the classroom, giving up this control is challenging. It often means accepting some chaos, making instructional missteps, and restructuring the way we approach teaching. It also has the potential to produce an existential crisis if we see ourselves as the leaders and directors in the classroom.

However, accepting this chaos and identity crisis (even in small ways) is also aligned with our ultimate goal for students: to develop independence, gain further control over their writing, and foster autonomy in critical thinking and learning. Even as we make mistakes and adapt to different students and contexts, we know conferencing is a more effective means to this end.

We started this process with our friend and colleague Christina Ponzio. Christina spent many years in the secondary ELA classroom. In the past, we presented with her at the National Council of Teachers of English on conferencing and other subjects. The genesis for this book was in one of those presentations. Christina has since gone on to pursue her PhD at Michigan State, but she helped launch us into this work with a review of the related research in the introduction.

Examples covered in this book represent actual lessons and practices we have tried; however, teacher and student names have been changed to maintain privacy. The opening anecdotes remain in the first person as our own reflections and experiences.

Acknowledgments

Many thanks to our colleagues who served as our first editors and readers: Christine Dawson, Natalie Novod, LaToya Patterson-Balzora, Jackie Pervizaj, and Christina Ponzio. We would also like to thank our co-teachers who help make conferencing possible: Nick Jacobson, Tanya Laloudakis, and Nina Thomas.

Introduction

Christina Ponzio

I struggled to see progress in my tenth grade English class. The students wrote, and I graded. What was missing? My feedback on every writing assignment was detailed, but an examination of student portfolios later in the year clearly showed the same feedback every time. The same problems occurred on almost every writing assignment. The cycle of writing and grading became increasingly frustrating and crushing to my confidence as a teacher. Did the students disagree with my feedback? Was the feedback overwhelming? The answer was actually more simple.

The students saw the submission of a writing assignment as the end of the process. If students looked through their graded essays at all, it was for the big letter written on the final page, not what I'd written throughout. It was not until I sat down and had impromptu meetings with the lowest-performing students that I realized how few of them read my feedback.

And if the students did read the feedback and had questions they wanted to ask me, their only opportunity was asking at the very end of the class period, when they were supposed to be elsewhere and I was meant to start the next class. Elementary school teachers and college writing workshop professors have known about and engaged with this problem for a long time. What they've realized: conversations are vital to students' growth as writers. —Anita

Young writers' identities and practices are best sparked and sustained within a "community of feedback," such as one-on-one writing conferences. Writing conferences have become a cornerstone in many language arts teachers' classrooms as an effective method to foster individualized student growth. Often conducted following short whole-class writing mini-lessons while students write independently, one-on-one writing conferences allow teachers to tailor their instruction to individual students' needs. At the secondary level, where teachers are responsible for twenty-two to thirty-four students each hour, writing conferences are one of the few opportunities students have to receive one-on-one instruction and support in the general education English language arts classroom.

WHY WRITING CONFERENCES?

As a pedagogical approach, conferencing provides an avenue for teachers to "apprentice" their students into how to talk about their own writing (Anderson, 2000, 2018; Calkins, 1994; Ray & Laminack, 2001). Students learn to look at their writing from the outside as well as how to talk about what they are doing—allowing them to take on the dual role of writer and audience and leading to more effective writing (Hawkins, 2016; National Writing Project, 2010; Tharp & Gallimore, 1991).

In addition, as students engage in conferences, they receive multiple models of how to talk with others about their writing, an important skill that may lead to more effective peer feedback and self-reflection (Anderson, 2000, 2018; Ray & Laminack, 2001). There is much to be said for the impact of a one-on-one conversation that weaves and moves in dynamic directions as opposed to the finality of red ink on a graded assignment.

Conferencing also sends an important message to students that they are in control of the writing process—not the teacher. In fact, one-on-one conferences create a context where teachers can engage students in goal setting and reflection (Baxa, 2015; Harford, 2008), provide timely feedback and strategies to develop self-regulation and error detection (Hattie & Timperly, 2007), and promote the "transfer of responsibility from teacher to learner" (Glasswell et al., 2003, p. 298).

When students believe they have ownership of their own writing, they can develop the habit of relying on what they know about writing rather than believing that the teacher is the ultimate authority and purveyor of grades. Removing the teacher as the sole expert in the room means feedback is not a dead end. Instead, feedback is an ongoing conversation in the course of a school year.

In what follows, I begin with an argument for enacting one-on-one conferences within the context of the writing workshop model. Time and time again, the writing workshop model has been found to be highly effective in engaging students in exploring writing genres and craft moves by emphasizing their agency in their own writing development (Anderson, 2000, 2018; Baxa, 2015; Calkins, 1994; National Writing Project, 2010; Ray & Laminack, 2001). As I will also discuss, one-on-one conferences are fundamental to creating a culture of growth and student ownership within the context of the writing workshop.

Next, I discuss why students need the opportunity to receive timely feedback and to take up that feedback with the support of a more experienced writer: their teacher. I conclude this introduction by identifying the key challenges secondary teachers face in enacting one-on-one conferences and outlining how this book will seek to address each of those challenges.

CONTEXTUALIZING CONFERENCES IN THE WRITING WORKSHOP MODEL

Learning to write in school-based contexts perpetuates a common misperception among students that writing is isolated within a short period of time during which they have to construct their piece for a very limited audience (the teacher) and purpose (the assignment). These limitations can decrease students' motivation during the writing process by making writing seem less authentic and meaningful (Coppola, 2017; Gallagher, 2015; Gallagher & Kittle, 2018). Furthermore, they can threaten the writer's identity by forcing his or her writing to conform to the box of a one-person audience—the teacher—who has framed the writing task with preestablished topics and who simply assigns a letter grade at the top of the piece of writing.

Instead, as Delpit (1988) suggests, "actual writing for real audiences and real purposes is a vital element in helping students to understand that they have an important voice in their own learning processes" (p. 33). Doing so communicates to students that their writing has real meaning—that their thoughts and ideas matter outside the four walls of the classroom. In contrast, the teacher's assignment threatens students' ownership of their writing by decreasing the level of autonomy students have over their writing. When constrained by predefined topics, guidelines, and deadlines, students tend to have little ownership over their writing and their writing process. Without the freedom to develop writing around interesting and engaging topics for a real audience and purpose, students' motivation to engage in writing is limited.

Writing workshops have become a mainstay in literacy education, emerging more than three decades ago as an instructional framework to apprentice young learners into the craft of writing, according to their interests and intentions for writing. The framework is based on four principles: students (1) write about their own lives, (2) use a consistent writing process, (3) work in authentic ways, and (4) develop independence as writers (Calkins, 1994; Calkins et al., 2005; Graves, 1983).

Within this framework, teachers model writing practices and strategies with short mini-lessons and provide additional guidance during one-on-one conferencing throughout the writing process (Calkins, 1994; Ray & Laminack, 2001). Through such workshops, the teacher acts as a mentor during the writing process, guiding the students' development of their writing through mini-lessons and conferences and providing them with the necessary support to become independent writers.

In the traditional writers' workshop, students have the opportunity to explore what other writers do. Often, teachers mediate this through the use of mentor texts that demonstrate the elements of effective writing and provide avenues for critiquing texts through large- and small-group discussions. By critically examining mentor texts, students have the opportunity to think about the craft of writing and how they apply what they learn to their practice.

Likewise, teachers use these mentor texts within short mini-lessons, where students receive direct instruction about strategies to try out in their own writing (Anderson, 2000, 2018; Calkins, 1994). These short lessons give students tools and strategies they can immediately apply to their writing—giving them hands-on experience as they develop their identities and practices as writers.

Providing students with one-on-one support through conferencing is fundamental to how teachers extend these mini-lessons and provide students with individualized support within the writing workshop model. In contrast to traditional practices within the secondary English context where feedback is unidirectional from teacher to student (often in the form of red-ink marginalia), one-on-one conferences provide teachers the opportunity to dialogue with students about where they are going as writers and how they will get there.

According to Murray (1985), conferences are "the working talk of fellow writers sharing their experience with the writing process" (p. 33). Through this talk, the teacher mentors students as writers, offering a new tool or strategy they can apply not only in that particular writing piece but also in their writing process as a whole.

But conferencing must also support students in developing greater independence in writing—where they do not need to depend on the teacher to shape their writing but gradually figure out how to do it themselves. That means that the focus needs to be on what will ensure each individual writer can grow in ways that expand beyond one piece of writing (Anderson, 2000, 2018; Calkins, 1994). Therefore, the purpose of such conferences is to get behind the work students are doing as writers and guide their development in writing practice in order to ensure the growth of both their writing pieces and their identities and skills as writers.

OVERVIEW OF THE BOOK

Given the affordances of student conferencing, it is no wonder that many educators, particularly at the elementary level, have adopted it as part of their writing pedagogy. However, secondary English teachers find themselves challenged to enact conferencing. With forty- to sixty-minute class periods and 125 or more students, middle and high school teachers face logistical constraints that limit their capacity to conduct meaningful conferences with individual students on a consistent basis.

Likewise, not only must adolescent writers be apprenticed into the craft of writing, but they must also learn the habits of thought, strategies, and skills to take ownership over their writing. So how do educators make conferences manageable, meaningful, and student driven in the secondary English classroom?

The purpose of this book is to share the inventive approaches the authors have developed to make conferences possible in the secondary English classroom. In chapter 1, they explore how to build a classroom culture that sustains one-on-one conferencing. This includes creating a community of practice where students have been apprenticed into the form of discourse and behaviors that invite them to take ownership of their own writing and support the writing practices of their classmates.

The next chapters share tools and examples that enact different types of conferencing, including the organizational systems and procedures needed to address the logistical challenges of one-on-one conferencing. The authors address common obstacles to conferencing, such as materials, classroom organization, the structure of class time, and what other students are doing (chapter 2). Then they discuss how to enact conferences before writing (chapter 3), during writing (chapter 4), throughout revision (chapter 5), and as a form of reflection with students' writing portfolios (chapter 6).

Included within each of these chapters are vignettes to illustrate how their ideas might be enacted and particular considerations to be made within each of these conference structures. In chapter 7, the authors take a step back to consider common challenges and constraints to enacting conferences. In the final part of the chapter, they offer resources for you to consider in planning your next steps to enact writing conferences in your classrooms and additional resources to make this possible.

Part I

Broader Context and Getting Started

ONE
Building a Culture of Conferencing

Marie has forgotten her vocabulary homework. Again. I ask her where it is, and all I get is an apathetic shrug. What the heck? How can I care more about her grades than she does? Later in the week, I find out Marie's family recently moved into a homeless shelter far from the school. I feel like such a jerk: how could I care about her vocab homework when she's dealing with so much more?

I regroup and try to focus on what I can control: a small slice of Marie's time in my classroom where I can provide structure and compassion. I can't solve larger problems, but where there is support, most academic concerns will fall into place. — Amy

There's so much beyond a teacher's control. It can feel overwhelming to adequately support the many aspects of students' academic, emotional, and mental well-being. The space in our classroom and the atmosphere created within it is perhaps the most important task to tackle. It is more crucial than any assessments or set of standards. A strong classroom culture creates the possibility for ambitious goals. Goals like attempting conferences in the secondary English classroom! But before getting to the nitty-gritty of conferencing practices, it's worth checking in to remember what factors nurture a productive atmosphere.

This chapter offers tips and suggestions for co-constructing classroom culture as the foundation for conferencing. The chapter begins by reviewing assignment ideas designed to establish a strong classroom culture from the beginning of the school year. For veteran teachers, these examples may offer additional ideas for practices that are already in place. For newer teachers, they could be a resource for getting started. Later, there are suggestions for maintaining and nurturing a classroom environment that supports conferencing as an ongoing pedagogical practice. Last, we consider how to segue from these assignments into the specific task of conferencing.

CRITICAL ATTRIBUTES: QUALITIES OF A STRONG CLASSROOM CULTURE

Even for veteran teachers, it is helpful to remember the key qualities of a strong classroom culture and consider what it should look like in practice.

Don't Make Assumptions: we all come to the classroom with different past experiences with education. For communities that have historically been underserved or subject to institutional racism, school does not represent a place of empowerment to attain success. We can serve students better when we are mindful of the multiple sources of stress they experience and see any potential reluctance or intransigence in a wider context.

Empathize: Our first reaction to students' defiance or frustration could easily be defensive or mirrored frustration. It can be easy to forget that we are all people in the world beyond the hour or less we share every day in the classroom. Recognizing that behavior is influenced by all these factors beyond the classroom and not taking behavior personally is crucial for building connections with students and making work productive.

Be a Model: The way we deal with confrontation, frustration, or tense moments in the classroom is a guide for how students should react in similar situations. Remain calm, retain a sense of humor, and keep an even keel to guide students for the behavior that is the expectation of everyone in the classroom.

Stay Positive: We create our own energy, and it is contagious. Giving students a clean slate every day they enter the classroom can be an emotional marathon, but it pays off for the culture it fosters. Greet students every day by their name. Welcome them back if they've been absent. Check that they're okay before chastising them for behavior. Give choices that demonstrate your concern rather than your irritation. It can take a lot of deep breaths to keep hiking the high road, yet it is a path worth taking.

Acknowledge Mistakes: Displaying our own missteps makes mistakes acceptable and even encouraged. Ask students' permission to try something new. Acknowledge it may not work. Talk through moments of frustration or lessons that end up as fiascos. The more we recognize our own shortcomings, the more these become permissible as learning opportunities.

Acknowledge and Celebrate: Validating students' frustration first before discussing an issue can go a long way in making them feel appreciated. Additionally, students have a range of dexterous expressions in informal and colloquial language that is not typically recognized in school. Code-switching to adapt language to a particular context takes lots of practice, and it can also be easy to forget how challenging it is. Making space to celebrate students' other "codes" through discussions, creative assignments (some of which are suggested in this chapter), and other venues gives this value and validation.

Nurture Constantly: We have so many things to do in any given school day; however, without this collaborative culture and engagement, productivity will diminish for any of them. Next, there are ideas to establish strong classroom culture on the first day. Later in this chapter, there are ideas for maintaining classroom culture beyond the first days of the school year.

STARTING THE YEAR OFF RIGHT: BUILDING CLASSROOM CULTURE FROM THE FIRST DAY

A nurturing, productive classroom culture begins the day classroom doors open for the new school year. Many teachers choose to start the year with activities or assignments that offer students the opportunity to share information or stories that highlight their personal background, interests, or concerns. Whatever their form, these assignments allow teachers to see students beyond their assigned seats, test scores, or student ID number. With the demands of prescribed curriculum, state tests, and other requirements, students rarely have the chance to share these more personal details in writing. Giving time and space for these assignments places value on the "whole" student and fosters their buy-in for anything else teachers hope to accomplish.

Conferencing affords substantial benefits, including placing the student in a more active role in receiving feedback and ideally taking more ownership of their learning. Similarly, when students feel valued, they are far more ready to step into this role, take conferencing more seriously, and engage with their own academic progress. Conferencing and classroom culture are therefore intricately tied, and we must support a strong culture before we can enter into meaningful conversations with students.

There are several options for assignments, activities, or projects that work well to set the tone of the year and give students a sense of their place in the classroom. The following assignments are from various middle and high school English classrooms; they could be adapted in length, focus, or substance as needed. Their most crucial aspect is that they showcase students as individuals and work to build trust in the classroom.

Greetings and Salutations: Using Letters to Introduce Yourselves

Ms. Cheng starts her eleventh grade AP English language class the first day with a letter to students. She introduces herself with pictures of her family and her pets. She also talks about her favorite books, hobbies, and how she spent her summer. She briefly introduces the course, then asks students to respond by sharing anything about their families, hobbies, or interests they would like to share. Finally, she asks students to tell her anything she should know about them as students and learners or ways to help them best. For example, Ms. Cheng suggests students may share nicknames, their seating preferences, and possibly their challenges with previous assignments or courses.

Finally, she often saves these letters and returns them to students at the end of the year, reflecting on how far they've come. Students are often shocked that a teacher can hold onto a piece of paper for an entire year, and they appreciate the letter was saved and looking back to where they began.

Example:

> Dear AP Language,
>
> Some of you I've met briefly, but for the most part I still need to get to know you. So I thought I would write you a letter to introduce myself. I've been teaching high school English for a long time. . . . Before coming to East-West, I taught at a public high school in the south Bronx. I love reading (of course), running, hiking, and swimming. I'm also the proud mom of a twelve-year-old girl, Cecilia; a ten-year-old boy, Matteus; and a six-year-old girl, Karina (check out pic below). This summer, we went on a massive road trip to see family and friends in Wisconsin (where I also went to college) and to camp in Yellowstone National Park. I came ten feet from running into a buffalo (!!) and saw some of the most beautiful landscape in our country.
>
> I am *very* excited to teach this class—studying rhetoric (the effective and purposeful use of language) can take many forms. We will analyze how writers, artists, filmmakers, advertisers, and others persuade us for different reasons. We'll also work on improving our own analytic and persuasive writing, skills that will serve you well in college and beyond. I have heard from Ms. Miller that you are great at debating, and I look forward to hearing your perspectives during our discussions. I expect college-level work from you in this course, a testament to your abilities, and likewise I hope to give you ample feedback on your writing.
>
> Now I want you to respond to me. I want at least one full page in response that gives me a brief picture of who you are as a person and a student. Please give me a paragraph or more for each of the following questions:
>
> 1. Tell me about yourself. Do you have any hobbies? Nicknames? Pastimes? Where is your family from? How many brothers and sisters do you have? Pets? Favorite book? Do you have any family members who attend(ed) this school? (You can choose to answer any combination of these questions; decide what you want to focus on.)

2. Is there anything I should know about you as a student to help you better? (For example, do you want to sit in the front, need extra help with reading assignments, prefer to be called a different name?)
3. What are your goals for this course? What do you hope to achieve (what strengths do you want to continue to improve, and what weaknesses do you hope to address in your reading or writing)? What are your goals for me?
4. What college majors or careers are you interested in? (I know it's still early to decide this, but I'm curious what you're thinking about.)
5. What questions or concerns do you have about the course or the AP exam? (I will be introducing both in more detail shortly, but let me know any specific questions.)

Looking forward to getting to know you and reading your letters.—Ms. Cheng

Excerpts from student letters:

"Since I have trouble seeing the board, I would like to sit closer to the front."

"As a student, I wouldn't consider myself as one of the best. I tend to struggle and not ask for help."

"I'm from Trinidad and Barbados. I have a lot of brothers and sisters. I do not like to read but if I had to it has to be a book about someone's life or a black history book."

"I have a turtle named Speedy and she is a very rude turtle."

"I would like to sit next to my good friend, Ryan Guitterez, and he is my spirit animal and emotional support."

Sharing Facets of Who We Are: Name Poems

Ms. Hill likes to open her seventh grade class with creative writing in the form of a poem. Students can write about their name, a hobby, or their family. While there are many online examples available, Ms. Hill prefers to use her own as a more powerful model for students to see. Sharing (appropriately) aspects of our personal lives opens the door for points of connection with students and creates an environment of safe exchanges. Further, this ideally creates a space where exposing vulnerability is accepted and encouraged.

Having a student write about the history of their name also acknowledges a breadth of experiences, familial connections, and cultural importance. Names signify a range of meanings within a culture, family, and social context. The different identifiers for ourselves might connect to community, geography, religion, family, friends, culture, profession, hopes, or fears. Honoring the complexity of these identifiers in writing (poem or otherwise) helps acknowledge their interconnectedness and provide a more comprehensive view of a young person beyond "student."

Sample #1:

> "Lily" has no special story.
> It's nice, but nothing new.
> A child born in April,
> Too early or too soon?
>
> Two weeks early, by my mother's count.
> I was made for May.
> Lily of the Valley, the May flower, perhaps.
> But April gave me daisies.
>
> Daisies are nice, but "Lily" means love,
> And innocence,
> And purity.
> But dictionary definitions don't define me.
> I'm not the delicate flower it makes me out to be.
>
> Like mother like daughter,
> She wanted me to be strong.
> "Lily" means justice,
> And determination,
> And truth.
>
> "Lily" is also simple,
> It's easy to say.
> Two syllables is all you need to express love.
> For my grandparents, anyway.
>
> Countless names passed their minds,
> Not "Sujin" or "Dahyun" or "Jiwoo"
> Not "Mei" or "Ling" or "Feng."
> Just one name will do,
> Not two or three.
> I am Lily, wherever I go,
> To everyone, I am me.

Sample #2:

> Her name had no origin. no justification. it was only supposed to be a form of identification in a new place that her parents only knew as 美国—the beautiful yet daunting land—which they were now supposed to call home and begin life **anew**.
>
> By the time she began questioning in a classroom filled with colorful boards and wooden tables pasted with stickers that read: Sophia, Anna, Sarah, she sought to fit in.

"Wen-nuh? Tell us about the origin of your name" was the typical icebreaker.

Too shy to explain it was Wee-nuh and hands sweating, face reddening, heart beating, none of the possible choices seemed to fit in; the "I was named after my grandpa" or the "my favorite great aunt named me" was the story she sought.

Instead, she turned to what she loved most: books. In a world where Cho Changs were admired, Eikko Koskinens were loved, and Lazlo Stranges were praised, she stumbled upon a word that resonated. **Anew: Wena backward.**

A·new -/əˈn(y)o͞o/ -adverb
in a new or different and typically more positive way.
"her self-reflection has begun anew, with accepting her name"

Her parents taught her to be independent, ambitious, and kind. What she thought was too much pressure and scolding was just love from another place of the heart. If she was a violin, her strings were broken, her pegs damaged, and her tone out of place.

She pledged that it was time to start **anew**. a fresh beginning that would put meaning into this four-letter identification.

*I am Wena, not Sophia, Sarah, or Anna and this is the story of my name which is yet to be written: a new chapter that has yet to begin **anew**.*

Sample #3:

"Being Unique"
Unique.
It's defined as an adjective,
"being the only one of its kind;
unlike anything else."

It's also . . . my middle name.

I think that was what
my mother was thinking
when I came out of the womb.
Or maybe even before that time,
when I was developing inside her.

She was probably thinking,
"This kid's gonna change the world."

"This kid of mine ain't gonna be
like the rest."
"This child of mine is gonna be different,
and I'm still gonna love him.
But he gotta know that his mama
is the most petty person on this planet!"

Trust me, I know that (NOW!)
And I also think you're right
about me being different from the rest.
Sometimes, our names do define us.
Other times, our name is just that:
A name.
Not an obligation, not a destiny
Just something that our parents thought
"What should this child be named?"
"What name should we present to the world?"

I think my mom gave me my name
because she knew that I was different.
Because she knew that I was gonna grow
and be someone who's going to
make a difference in this world;
to make lives better, and make people
happy.
She probably thought of that definition
of what it means to be UNIQUE
And she decided
To give me that name.
A name that I'm going to keep
All the way to my grave.

Sample #4:

Lie-ZA. it tastes so bitter. *Lie-ZA*. A curse, a stranger.

A long time ago, her name was indisputable. Nowadays it is up to luck, the weather, and God if someone gets it right. Her name is dying, but how do you lose a name?

"Lie-za?"
"Lisa, with a z"
"But that's not how we say it"

I own my name, it is mine and not yours. A chant, a reminder. Liza [lisa], Liza [lisa]. the sky is blue and I am Liza [lisa].

> A latino name? Spanish pronunciation? I don't need to justify my name to you.
> this gift given to me for simply living. My first gift forged by love, never inherited. There's no legacy, no stories. Not yet.
>
> Liza [lisa]. Lisa but that s is too soft yet the z too sharp. Say it right. Write it well. *This is my name.*

Picture It: Graphic Novels of Family Histories

In an eleventh grade American literature class, Ms. Thomas starts the year off asking students to write a graphic novel. Using Gene Yang's *American Born Chinese* as a shared text and loose guide, students tell their family's history in America. Ms. Thomas also created a model with her own family's story of coming to America from India. Students can focus on the influence of an important family member, the story of how their parents met, their family's immigration story, or the description of important holidays in their family (among other potential topics). The final product includes a cover page, a one-page written explanation of their novel's story, and four pages of art. Telling their own family's story of living in America dovetails into discussions of themes in American literature, including the immigration experience, the American dream, and the formation of an American identity. These themes not only are part of the course's reading but also weave through the students' own stories. Making these connections explicit helps students gain access to the curriculum and feel valued within it.

Share It: Putting It on Display

Each of these assignments (letters, name poems, or graphic novels) focuses on valuing the student as a person before turning to academic concerns. Teachers' sharing their own examples of these assignments helps establish trust and build the teacher–student relationship. Sharing personal information fosters a context where vulnerability is accepted, mistakes are permissible, and risk taking is welcomed.

Exchanging these assignments early in the year in a public way (gallery walk, bulletin boards, stations) amplifies students' voices and makes them feel valued in the classroom space. Gallery walks display work around the room that students visit, possibly taking notes. Stations might have a few works at every table that students visit for a few minutes at a time, then rotate. Even students who seem apathetic and unengaged notice whose work is on the bulletin board. To that end, this validation through public display can also help encourage reluctant or unmotivated students to stay focused and keep making progress. Finally, students feel

Figure 1.1. Sample of student graphic novel Photo by Amy Matthusen

more ownership of the classroom space when it is filled with their own work.

KEEP THE BALL ROLLING: NURTURING CULTURE THROUGHOUT THE YEAR

A strong classroom culture needs tending and care to thrive. Establishing a good rapport and productive classroom at the beginning of the year is only useful when it is consistently maintained. The goals and values established early in the year will need revisiting and ongoing discussion, or the unaddressed fissures related to classroom routines start to crack and crumble. The suggestions below offer ideas and reminders to foster and maintain positive culture in the classroom throughout the year.

The Power of Praise

The students and the assignments we praise offer their own lessons in showing students what is valued in our classrooms. Equitable acknowledgment among different populations of students is crucial. However, teachers should also carefully consider *what* is praised. In the current

Figure 1.2. Sample of student graphic novel Photo by Amy Matthusen

high-stakes-testing environment of schools, it is important to remember to acknowledge not just academic achievement but growth and effort as well. Remembering this growth is essential in conferencing conversations, which offer opportunities to recognize students' specific examples of growth in writing and efforts to improve.

Other potential examples of praise are bulletin boards and awards teachers may offer to students. While some students may feel self-conscious about the attention, most will be thrilled at the recognition. Rather than post polished final drafts from high-performing students, bulletin boards (or their like) can offer space to display growth across different stages of an assignment. For example, we can choose to highlight how a student has incorporated feedback and progressed. This growth is just as noteworthy as high achievement, and our recognition demonstrates this. Making this explicit to students sustains classroom culture, empowers students, and bolsters the work done in individual conferences.

Take a Seat and Ask a Question

We all face irritations during the school year from any number of factors. At some point in the year, the accumulation of small grievances between students and teachers will lead to frustration. It is easy to lose

Figure 1.3. Sample of student graphic novel Photo by Amy Matthusen

sight of students as individuals and only see the specific problems they pose in class—missing homework, lack of motivation, or even defiance. Ms. Patterson is a classroom culture master. Frustrated by a student's behavior, she offered some of the best advice we've heard: "Take a seat and ask a question."

So simple and so genius. Sit down next to students at their eye level—a deft teacher move that in itself levels the playing field to give dignity and respect to the student. Don't judge. Don't assume. Ask. Acknowledge. *You seem frustrated. What's going on? How can I help?* Become an ally, not an antagonist. Moves so simple we forget them. Yet they lie at the heart of any healthy relationship and can be our best resources throughout the school year for maintaining productive and engaged classroom culture where students feel valued. Also, be sure to speak with a variety of students so no one student feels singled out.

The Workshop Model

One of the ways to prepare a class for a culture of conference is the workshop model. The model includes a mini-lesson of the day's skill, a model of the task, and then an opportunity for work. Students need time to process and practice. In this environment, there is an expectation of

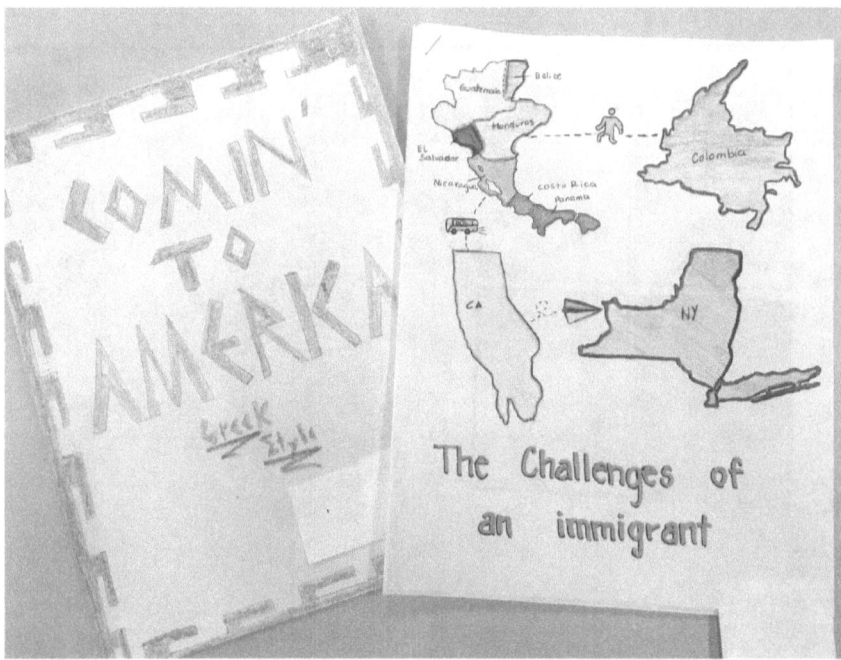

Figure 1.4. Sample of student graphic novel Photo by Amy Matthusen

time for independent, pair, or group work. The workshop model acclimates students to a student-centered model where the teacher does not spend the class period engaged in chalk and talk; rather, it encourages accountability by allowing space to work.

A workshop-model classroom hinges on the idea that instructors can step away from being the nucleus of the classroom in order to observe, assess, and assist as needed during the work period. Certainly, not every lesson is conducive to the workshop model; however, the benefit of a workshop model once or twice a week in a classroom cannot be overstated. In a conferencing culture, an instructor feels comfortable conducting meetings with students on the periphery while the rest of the students work either on related writing tasks or other tasks entirely. Not all conferences can be done while the rest of the class is also doing a part of the same assignment. Some conversations need to occur in the daily grind, perhaps by fitting in one student in a period—just for a few minutes.

Show Yourself as a Writer

While it is incorrect to assume that all English teachers want to be writers, it is true that all English teachers write. Yet we forget to share that aspect of our lives. Teachers write emails, proposals, and profession-

Figure 1.5. Bulletin board featuring growth and progress Photo by Amy Matthusen

al development presentations, perhaps in addition to personal writing. For students to understand that writing is an ongoing process that benefits from peer review and repeated reflection, students need to see instructors' writing.

At the beginning of the year, when students are writing the name poems, so should the teacher. Obviously, this is a way to share aspects of oneself; however, a more impactful presentation of the teacher's poem is to watch the teacher create the poem in front of students. How many words were discarded before the perfect word was selected? Which phrase captured the overall intended mood?

For initial longer writing assignments, complete the prompt. Then hand over the prompt and the assignment to another teacher to "grade" and provide feedback. Consider even recording a conversation between yourself and your peer so students observe the nonpunitive nature of conferences and the dynamic nature of conversation. Present the peer review (written or visual) and your process of revising an aspect of the writing in class. If a peer review is not possible, then complete a think-aloud: verbalize the changes and make these thoughts explicit so students see the process. This seems simplistic, but later conferences between the student writer and the instructor hinge on trust and a welcoming atmosphere.

In a class that is preparing for a timed writing exam, a teacher sitting down to complete a timed prompt *with* students can be humbling and illuminating. After the writing, talk through the experience with students. Don't focus on the product; focus on the process. What was difficult? Did your hand start to cramp? How did you deal with a good idea that came to you partway through your writing?

Show students that you likely faced the same challenges they will. In this scenario, it is less important to model a product than to build camaraderie as a community of writers. Teachers are now allies in a process rather than dictators of standards, which has a significant effect on the classroom's culture.

Keep "Taking the Temperature"

As teachers, we're used to telling students how they're doing. In Ms. Christiansen's ninth grade English class, she builds in time throughout the year to "take the temperature" of her classroom. She uses this opportunity to measure how students are feeling and gauge the effectiveness of lessons or the clarity of instruction. Asking students gives us valuable feedback on lessons to improve instruction and foregrounds student voice. Many of these practices are easy to streamline into lessons and classroom practices.

For example, students often write exit tickets to measure content knowledge or ask a lingering question. These could easily include a question related to how they are doing: *On a scale from one to five (one feeling good, five not so hot), how are you feeling about class right now? Do you feel you can succeed in this class? Explain.* When students are working in small groups, pairs, or even independently, teachers usually circulate. Stopping to sit down next to an individual or group of students is a move that opens a conversation for more attentive listening. In a hectic classroom, we are often challenged to really listen. Just making this a more explicit and conscious practice to "take the temperature" can shift a culture by small degrees to make eventual major shifts. Finally, adding a question to homework, written response, or other assignment that is related to students expressing concerns is also a form of this "listening" to provide similar benefits. The "emoji exit" ticket in the figure is another example of a quick check-in to see how students are feeling.

Take a Break

Sometimes the best way to regroup a class is to (shh!) completely step away from academics. Play a game; watch a video. If it's a viable option, go outside. The connection to content can still be there, but the break in

Figure 1.6. Emoji exit ticket *Directions:* **Circle the emoji above that best reflects how you feel about what we covered in class today. Then write two to three sentences explaining your choice.**

the routine and camaraderie offered can be rejuvenating, especially in the long stretches between vacations or the hectic schedules of the school year.

PIVOTING FROM CULTURE TO CONFERENCING: STARTING THE CONVERSATION

After sharing assignments designed to acknowledge students' unique backgrounds, teachers can then transition to engaging students as readers and writers in the classroom. In the context of an inclusive classroom culture, these early conversations can segue to more explicit academic concerns. At this point, students can consider their own goals as readers and writers as they align with the course's content and expectations, and potentially share these goals with their peers and teachers.

Classroom and school rules are more meaningful and sustainable when they are student generated and reflect students' voices. Similarly, writing goals carry more weight and are more viable when students articulate for themselves how they would like to improve as writers. Some goals may include improving organization, style, thesis statements, vocabulary, development, or any other aspect of various genres. By asking students to drive the goals of the writing process, teachers demonstrate that they value them as writers who can steer the direction of this work. Rather than dictate demands, teachers become a source of support.

The example below is one method of polling students to better understand their concerns as writers and give students agency in how they receive feedback. Regardless of how this type of assignment is organized, it is useful if the teacher reviews the types of feedback students typically receive on their writing and asks students to express their preferences for how they receive feedback.

Student Surveys

After giving his Google Form survey (or any other similar survey tool), Mr. Dawson shares the collective results with his students. Based on past experience, he knows his class will likely select "individual conferences" as their general preference for feedback because students appreciate the individual attention conferences provide as well as the clarity of feedback in conversation (as opposed to written feedback).

Mr. Dawson's Eighth Grade Writer Survey (Given as a Google Form)

1. What is your name?
2. What period of English are you in (select)?
3. What kind of writing are you interested in working on (add selections depending on course)?
4. Explain your answer above.
5. What are some aspects of your writing you are interested in improving?
6. How do you prefer to receive feedback (select any from below: general comments to the class, marks on rubric, individualized written feedback, individualized conference with teacher)?
7. Explain your answer above.

Mr. Dawson then discusses the benefits and challenges of conferences. For most students, the individual attention and feedback can be highly impactful for students' writing. Students are active in the conversation about their work rather than the passive recipients of written feedback where there is no space for their voices. Conferences, as we know, pose significant logistical challenges in keeping a whole class focused while the teacher is working with one student. With this in mind, Mr. Dawson turns the discussion back to the students and asks, How do we get this done?

Mr. Dawson divides the class into thirds. Each small group is tasked with establishing a set of expectations for each party: teacher, students in conferences, and students in class during conferences. Similar to how many teachers begin the year with students creating or guiding a set of class rules, Mr. Dawson extends this idea to the specific practice of conferencing.

This task could be set up in different ways using poster paper, shared Google Docs, or stations. Groups of four or five students come up with the expectations for a teacher, a student in a conference, or students outside the conference. In a larger class, there could be two small groups with the same focus and ideas combined later. In a shared space, the class can display their notes for all to see. Or a shared document could be displayed on a smart board. On paper, they could be displayed with a document camera, or made into posters and placed at the front of the room.

With this brainstorming on display (likely similar to the examples below), the expectations could be transferred into a more formal text that becomes the class's guide for each participant's responsibility. Since these are student generated, there should be more buy-in for students' own responsibility, preparation, and focus for the practice of conferencing.

Mr. Dawson's Student-Generated Conference Expectations

The teacher should

- Come prepared with materials and resources for the conference
- Listen to students' concerns
- Give clear advice and suggestions
- Give each student equal time

The student in the conference should

- Come prepared
- Ask questions
- Listen with an open mind

Students in class should

- Focus on work (you do not want your own conference interrupted by a distracted or loud class)
- Save a question for later—email or write it on a Post-it
- See if a peer can help if necessary

SUMMARY

Key steps to establishing a strong classroom culture include the following:

- Getting to know students in a personal way
- Helping students establish individual goals as readers and writers
- Establishing clear expectations for conferences for teachers, students conferencing, and students in class during conferences

- Valuing progress, not perfection
- Consistently nurturing to maintain productivity

TWO
Getting Organized and Overcoming the Biggest Hurdles

Sometime back, I was the teacher's helper in my daughter's classroom. The third graders were working on a writing and art project. I was assigned the group of students creating cover art, but I grew increasingly distracted and awed by what was happening around me. There were groups of students all around the room working on different aspects of the project while the teacher was simply at her desk conferencing with one student. I did not catch her getting up and instructing students to move on to this or that. Some children were still working on the first version of a memoir. Some were putting the finishing touches on a revised version, while others were doing cover art with me. I was humbled. How is this level of coordination and self-regulation occurring in elementary classrooms but not in my ninth and tenth grade high school classroom? — Anita

Conferences seem to be a natural component of an elementary classroom because there is only one set of students all day long. The student number appears manageable, and there is flexibility to adjust the schedule of the day according to the needs of the assignment. This is in stark contrast to middle and high school classrooms, in which students might seek out the teacher before or after school, but most often during lunch, to have a conversation about their writing, since there seems to be a lack of time in the class period. The conversations are too often hurried and lacking in a systematic method of recording the back-and-forth between the student and the teacher.

There are a seemingly endless number of activities and daily protocols teachers would attempt if, and only if, the organization did not appear too cumbersome. The high school classroom library? Oh, what a lovely idea for every teacher except the one who travels room to room. A quiet corner for students to decompress on a bean bag? Perhaps not when space is at a premium in a thirty-two-student classroom. Conferencing appears to be one of those ideas that teachers *know* to be effective but refrain from implementing due to concerns about time constraints, classroom management, and fruitful implementation.

Unique school, classroom, and curriculum demands create obstacles to spending individual time with students. Clear expectations and consistent protocols can, however, produce a class of independent students and teachers with time to meet individually. Rather than a one-way delivery of feedback to passive recipients, these conferences promote students as directors of a dialogue that leads to greater ownership of progress. Conferences offer a meaningful space where students take more significant strides if we utilize the tools and practices that make this work possible. The first steps are getting organized and considering strategies to overcome the challenges of conferences with students in a secondary setting.

WHAT MATERIALS DO I NEED TO GET STARTED?

Systems to Track Progress

One of the benefits of conferencing is the product at the end of the year that contains all the notes about a student's progress. An Excel or Google Sheets file is the best way to track. For each class, create a simple list of students' names running vertical. On the horizontal include the dates of meetings and assignments. In addition, if possible, other information can be included, such as reading levels or last state standardized exam results. The columns of information can include anything that provides a quick picture of the student at a glance.

At the beginning of the school year, it is unlikely that any teacher knows their students well. These trackers could contain information on interests or how the student views reading and writing. Such information can be extracted through surveys or handwritten "About Me" letters, as discussed in the previous chapter.

Most teachers teach five classes that contain anywhere from twenty-five to thirty-two or more students each. While the addition of the more personal information might appear to be excessive work in the chaos of the first month of the school year, it pays dividends later in conferences. The teacher can quickly refer to the information before the conference starts in earnest and tailor questions to make the student more comfortable.

Student Name	Info reading level/ interest/ misc	Student's Questions	Antigone Essay Feedback	Teacher Name	Othello Outline Question/ Feedback	Teacher
Jason	3/ skateboards/ last year attendance problem	says has not questions, has no problems.	summary not in order. Body paragrahs not focused. Missing third body intro. Body1: Antigone and why she wants to bury her brother importance of family and not being scared of dying. Body2: Haiom takes Antigones side.. explain why and how he reject his the king and laws. Body #3: Creon stands by his law and he loses his wife and son.	Abraham	12/18- Topic 3 outline. Good thesis. Focus is Iago. Needed help not repeating the thesis.	Abraham
Karla	2/ taught brother also/ says no hobbies	links	Changed topic sentences and thesis- told to find stronger evidence	Abraham	Did not complete outline - asked for help with thesis- might need more help as year progress on thesis formulation	Abraham
Jane	2/ likes math	topic sentence	topic sentences were fine. Told to research. interesting ideas and flow	Abraham	12/18- Needed ideas for paragraphs- unable to brainstorm ideas unless someone speaks with her / 12/20- had a typed essay but each paragraph missing evidence- said she is looking-- seems to want to organize thoughts before finding proof	Abraham

Fig. 2.1. Tracker example

During the student and teacher conference, the teacher makes notes on current progress, struggles and gains the student shares, and next steps. Also of note are skill deficiencies or misconceptions that multiple students have. Which students could be grouped together for a more efficient group conversation later? The horizontal manner of tracking allows for a quick perusal of issues resolved or unresolved. An examination of the vertical sheds light on whole-class issues.

For every assignment, the teacher will not see every student at every stage. Maintaining a spreadsheet allows for observations about which students like to be seen at different stages of the writing process. Patterns will emerge that will provide data about which students could be brought together for group conferencing or work on a particular skill.

Portfolios

Portfolios, whether online or physical, are a necessity in a classroom where reflection is continual.

Students may keep an online portfolio either in Google Classroom or on Turnitin.com. This enables easy access for the student and teacher.

Technology may be temperamental at times. For conversations, hard copies of assignments are preferable. Have every student bring to class a two-pocket folder to house their writing. It is easier to view progress over the course of the year when assignments may be spread out. The student folder stays in class, and each period may be housed in a separate basket.

Students should also have a way to manage and track the conferences. Have students place in their folder a sheet as a student tracker, or create an online document. The information to include: date, assignment, stage of writing, notes from conference, and next steps.

The sheet is part of the portfolio of work that the student has access to. While individual assignment feedback and rubrics include next steps, tracking on one sheet multiple writing pieces enables the student to see how next steps and skills shift throughout the year. In a way, it acts as a checklist of accomplishments and further actions. What used to be a problem? What is still an issue?

Maintaining a portfolio makes goal setting and reflection easier. Students should set goals a few times in the year, typically at the beginning of marking periods or units. At a minimum, these could occur at the beginning of the year (self-identified strengths, weaknesses), in the middle of the year (gains and new concerns), and as a final reflection at the end of the year. The questions could be written answers or boxes students check off. Again, these can be low-tech paper surveys or high-tech Google Forms. The benefit of Google Forms is the chance to see trends within classes and among classes.

Encourage students to see writing as a continual work in progress. Let them know you do not expect perfection. A way to model this is to share your own writing. *Here is what I was trying to do. Here is my feedback and what I did in response. I make errors, I change my mind, and I refine.*

Students like to collect their work and see the progress over time. Provide opportunities to look at the work in their portfolio. Ask them to write notes to themselves on Post-its attached to their older writing. *What do I see? What do I not do anymore? I wrote this sentence well. I'm impressed with how much I've grown.*

Allow students to view each other's portfolios. Make it a publishers' party where the objective is to compliment. It is human nature to point out what is not working in our own writing. It is validating to see our work and effort through someone else's eyes.

Finally, encourage students to see their grade as dependent on progress. If students realize that the end-of-semester conferencing means a chance to improve their grade and an opportunity to advocate for themselves, they buy into the process.

Sign-Up Sheets

Ron is a student who wants frequent feedback. With this desire comes multiple conversations with Ms. Jemson. Each revision is printed and brought to the teacher's attention. In Mrs. Abraham's co-taught class, Ron also seeks feedback from the ENL (English as a new language) teacher, Mr. Rhi. While this level of commitment is admirable, it takes away from other students' conversation time with teachers. There is an obvious solution: sign-up sheets. Ms. Jemson's solution was a large sign-up sheet. Each day, the giant sign-up sheet served to inform the students who had conferences when and with which teacher in the co-taught classroom.

A simple online sign-up sheet, such as a Google Sheets file, shared with the students through Google Classroom, is another way to manage student conferences and minimize repeat visitors (see figure 2.2). It establishes set times and an understanding that, though the meetings happen in class, it is an appointment with a set beginning and ending. As such, no student should encroach upon the time of another. It is worthwhile to discuss the value of respecting each other's time. Breaking up the scope of conferences over more days, with instruction in between, is also a strategy to vary structure and make conferencing less overwhelming.

Timers

Timers are the merciless machines of equality. There is always that one student who has too many questions and does not grasp the idea that other students also need access. Just like a child anxious for one-on-one time with parents, so a student can be possessive of time with the instructor. Teachers want to provide all the time the student desires, but it is difficult to say that time is up. The timer does the awkward work. The

Sample calendar and sign-up sheet:

Mon. Jan. 6: Scarlet Letter reading journal pages 141-161 **responses due**
Tues. Jan 7: prose practice: read, annotate, create thesis statement [prep for timed essay Th!] + MP conferences
Wed. Jan. 8: Scarlet Letter reading journal pages 161-169 **responses due**; finish book & email question
Th. Jan. 9: timed prose essay + Marking Period conferences
Fri. Jan. 10: vocab quiz; multiple choice practice + Marking Period conferences

Mon. Jan. 13: small group discussion
Tues. Jan. 14: prepare written discussion question responses + Marking Period conferences
Wed. Jan. 15: final Scarlet Letter discussion
Th. Jan. 16: TBD: multiple choice practice/or poem response + Marking Period conferences
Fri. Jan. 17: Marking Period 3 ends; review for mock exam

Please sign up for an MP conference in the grid below*; review questions and come prepared for our conversation. Failure to adequately prepare for the conference will be reflected in your final grade.
*Note: When the grid is full, three students will need to make arrangements with me to meet outside of class.

Date/time	9:40-9:50	9:50-10:00	10:00-10:10	10:10-10:20
Tues. Jan. 7				
Th. Jan. 9				
Fri. Jan. 10				
Tues. Jan. 14				
Th. Jan. 16				

Figure 2.2.   Sign-up sheet

timer could be a phone application or a physical timer. Either way, the timer establishes boundaries that clearly indicate the start and end of a conversation.

Plan to spend five minutes in conversation with a student during a class period. If the class period is longer than the typical forty-five minutes, then the conversation could be longer. Plan to be equitable. There are students for whom five minutes is four minutes too long to engage in a conversation about their writing with a teacher. Resist the urge to let the student go on his or her way. The awkward silence will be filled. Ask questions when they do not have questions or concerns. Push and prod because the student is entitled to their full time even if the first few times conferring is painful for the student and the teacher.

HOW DO I ORGANIZE THE CLASSROOM?

The organization of the class depends on student number and space. There is not a special way to set up a classroom; however, be cognizant of the need to conduct a conference while engaged in active classroom management.

The teacher's desk could be the location of the conference. The desk should be placed in such a way that a quick glance during a conference provides the teacher a full view of the classroom. It is easier to manage student work from the back of the classroom rather than the front. It is easy to hide phones behind books when the teacher is facing the students. The teacher's desk should be a little away to give the suggestion of privacy.

If space is not a limited commodity, consider a conference area that is not at the teacher's desk. The desk confers on the teacher the aura of expertise, which in turn could cause a student to be more reticent. In elementary classrooms, teachers use a separate (usually circular) desk that is free of the detritus of teaching to meet with students. Also, consider a desk that is higher (like a bar table and stool), which allows for a bird's-eye view of the class. A separate space for conferencing can create intimacy without compromising management.

In addition, leverage seating assignments; possibly have higher-needs students closer to the teacher conference area. Students who have trouble with task initiation and stamina need to be closer also for less intrusive classroom management.

Consider also thoughtful grouping. Not all tasks need to be silent and independent. Students may be temporarily working on either homogeneous or heterogeneous work depending on the objectives of the lesson and task.

Timers writ large on smart boards reinforce that tasks have deadlines. There is no need for repeated interruptions from the teacher indicating how much time is left to create a sense of urgency. Next to the timers, the tasks can be broken down in list form to help students manage their time and convey expectations about noise level.

HOW DO I STRUCTURE CLASS TIME?

Planning is vital to allow sufficient class time for both conferences and writing. Consider the entire unit and the summative assignment. How many students need to be seen? And, realistically accommodating for interruptions and classroom management, how much time could be allotted to each child at the different stages of writing?

A class of thirty cannot be seen in less than three periods. Seeing every child means allowing for roughly four minutes a student. For specific assignments, as opposed to conferences about semester and end-of-year grades, there is no need to see every student. See the student at the stage of writing that he or she needs most assistance with. In this way, all students are spoken to without the pressure of seeing everyone all at once. Why waste time conferencing about planning and introduction with a student who needs more help with analysis or revision?

In addition, when planning class time, think about which groups of students could be seen together. Prior assignments provide data on similar skill deficiencies that could be addressed in small group settings.

Timers are a teacher's best friend. An active timer informs students that their time is valuable but not infinite. Time is limited for both parties, which means the other students are not wondering if they will be seen that period. Timers also impart a sense of urgency that is less abrasive than a teacher saying, "We are almost out of time!" and "Now we are out of time!"

For end-of-semester or end-of-year conversations, ten minutes is a rough estimate for the conversation. The timer prohibits, in a way, the teacher from rushing through the conversation to get to the next student. For a student, ten minutes in one-on-one conversation seems like an eternity. However, it is an eternity they may use to advocate for themselves. Awkward, sure, the first time they do it; better every time after.

Middle school and high school have different time constraints since some middle schools often have double periods. The double period might seem like a built-in bonanza of time; however, there might be issues maintaining the interest and focus of the students not in a conference. Conferences could occur at different times in the double period. Perhaps a group of students at the beginning of class, followed by teacher-led instruction for the whole class, and then another group of students for conferences toward the end of the double period.

Later chapters will discuss how to manage students at different stages of writing with specific types of conferences.

WHAT SHOULD A CONFERENCE LOOK LIKE?

Fishbowl a Conference as a Model

Before conferencing, consider performing a mock conference with an outgoing student in a "fishbowl." Let the class use the conference grading criteria (see figure 2.3). Teacher and student meet ahead of time to discuss what they will say in general. The student can bring a piece of writing they are working on, seeking advice, asking questions, and planning next steps. Teacher and student can sit in the middle of the classroom (the "fishbowl"). Observing students can sit in a circle around the conference, taking notes on a two-column page, writing down "teacher moves" and "student moves" in either column. Outside students could also use a conference rubric to evaluate strengths and weaknesses of the conversation.

After the mock/model conference, the instructor could engage in a whole-class discussion to break down what the students noticed about the conversation: What was the student doing? How did he or she use evidence or preparation? What could improve? What are the student writer's next steps? How are the teacher and student tracking this? Making these qualities of the conference explicit to students helps make expectations clear, eases student anxieties, and leads to better conferences. Additionally, grading the conference itself can create a greater sense of value, importance, and buy-in for students' preparation.

Running a Mock Conference to Generate Criteria

With the goals of the conference in mind, teachers may also consider doing a strong and weak mock conference in front of the class, asking students to note what they see. The teacher can ask students to evaluate the conference: what made the conversation stronger or weaker? Soliciting responses in discussion and posting answers on the board could then be compiled into student-generated conference criteria based on the mock examples (likely producing similar criteria). This may further invest students in the process since they created the criteria by which they are evaluated. Making the conference its own assignment and highlighting the qualities of a strong conference invests students in the process and ideally provides a more enriching conversation for a stronger future product.

HOW DO I TRAIN THE CLASS TO LET US TALK?

Culture Culture Culture

Before any set of conferences can successfully begin, it is crucial to establish and nurture a classroom culture to support this work. With the demands of a busy school year, practices and explicit conversations about culture are easy to put off or set aside. Yet they are crucial for productive work. Why is this valuable to us as a class and you as a writer? If you (student) value my undivided attention when we are in conversation, how should you extend the same expectations to your work when you are not in a conference? Chapter 1 offers specific ideas to create and foster a positive classroom culture to help support this work.

Outside Questions during Conferences

Even with a strong classroom culture, this work is difficult, especially with a single teacher in a large class of potentially struggling students. There are, however, strategies to make conferences possible even on a smaller scale. Establishing clear expectations and procedures well before conferences begin will eliminate many of the potential interruptions during conference time.

Conference Grading Criteria

A (90-100):
- Arrives punctually (or even early) for scheduled conference time
- Demonstrates thorough preparation with use of all necessary materials (outline, text, any supplemental work)
- References specific work/materials throughout conversation
- Asks specific questions for clarification, further instruction, or improvement
- Has substantive written answers to conference questions

B (80-89):
- Arrives punctually for scheduled conference time
- Demonstrates adequate preparation with some use of most materials (outline, text, any supplemental work)
- References specific work/materials during conversation
- Asks some questions for clarification, further instruction, or improvement
- Has adequate written answers to conference questions

C (70-79):
- May arrive late for scheduled conference time
- Demonstrates some preparation with materials, but could be more substantial or developed
- References specific work/materials minimally during conference conversation
- Questions are basic, and could be more detailed or reflective
- Written answers to conference questions could be more detailed or complete

D (60-69):
- May arrive late for scheduled conference time
- Demonstrates minimal preparation
- May lack necessary materials
- Lacking thoughtful questions
- Written answers to conference questions demonstrate minimal effort, or left incomplete

Figure 2.3. Conference grading criteria

Nonetheless, issues will likely still arise. Establish a procedure for these smaller interruptions to protect conference time and allow students to remain productive. A teacher may give Post-it notes to students and have a poster or board space designated as a "Parking Lot" to post questions. The teacher can address these when it is convenient, or possibly the following day at the beginning of class. Another option for dealing with students' outside questions during conferences is using digital tools like Poll Everywhere, Today's Meet, or ProProfs. Sites like these create virtual spaces for students to ask questions. A teacher could have this open on a laptop during a conference, or you could create a space where students answer and help each other as they work and you conference.

Incentivize Students' Work outside Conferences

Creating and maintaining a classroom that supports conferencing takes time and constant attention to develop the practice and maintain mutual respect. It is tempting to grade outside students' behavior and penalize them for being off task. While this is a potential solution, it can be detrimental to the wider classroom culture as penalized students feel frustrated with the process rather than incentivized to contribute to a practice that should ultimately benefit them during their own conference time.

Avoid busy work, which can quickly lead to students losing focus. Instead, teachers are better served by creating meaningful high-stakes work for students outside of conferences (discussed in more detail later in this chapter). If possible, grade this work quickly so students see its value. In other parts of this book, there are also suggestions for assignments during conference time. The details and focus of these assignments are largely dependent on individual teacher contexts. Whatever their focus, this work should be meaningful, related by content or skills to the course, and tied to grades so its value is clear.

HOW DO I SEE EVERY STUDENT FOR A CONFERENCE?

Dividing Students and Conferences across the Writing Process

In the secondary classroom, it can be very challenging to try and see the hundred or more students teachers work with, especially if there is only one instructor in the classroom. Many teachers would like to see students after they have finished a draft of a writing piece and before revision. This is an ideal time for the conversation but nearly impossible logistically.

This work becomes more manageable, however, when we divide the conversations across the writing process and see fewer students over a longer period of time. There are also options to help when instructors consider technological tools, utilize co-teachers, or consider small-group conferencing. Each of these is discussed in more detail with examples in other parts of this book.

Additionally, in each chapter of this book, there are strategies to consider specific students to target at different phases of the writing process. Candidates for early conferencing are English language learner (ELL) students who may have misunderstood the task and writers who need an initial push to get over the daunting task of just starting. Students who are perfectionists and are afraid of making any initial mistakes may also benefit from early conversations during brainstorming and outlining. During the drafting phase, it is helpful to see students who want to check if they are on the right track, need encouragement to keep up, or struggle with stamina in writing.

In revision conferences, teachers may choose to see students who started but were unable to finish their first draft. Students who want to verbalize concerns they came upon while writing or those who need help seeing their own strengths also benefit from a conference at this stage. Finally, reflective or portfolio conferences could help students see the value of process over product. These conversations also help student writers who benefit from seeing the larger picture of smaller assignments across the year or discouraged students who may not initially recognize the progress they have made.

Every student writer can benefit from individual conferences at any stage of the writing process. When instructors know their classes well, they can consider which students to see at which phase, maximizing both their time and effort most effectively. This then affords the possibility of making conferences more manageable as we are not attempting to see every student at the same time.

WHAT OTHER RESOURCES CAN I USE TO CONFERENCE WITH MORE STUDENTS?

Co-teachers

For classrooms with more than one teacher, leveraging two instructors can be a game-changing option to allow conferences to become part of the practice and routines to serve students. With one teacher leading class, another teacher might be able to pull out targeted students for conversation.

Monitoring student focus is far easier with another set of eyes, and the additional teacher is another resource for students. Working out ahead of time who assumes which role and what the expectations are for each instructor keeps the focus clear and allows for equitable distribution of leadership, course direction, and assessment of student learning. Having two teachers conducting conferences speeds up the process when students realize both teachers have the expertise to assist them.

Here is the rub: If you do not provide co-teachers space in the classroom as both a voice and an authority, then do not expect them to assist with conferences. Students will not want to address writing issues with a teacher who appears not to have power. Special education and ELL teachers approach writing tasks differently from English teachers. Special education teachers understand how different students learn, break down tasks, evaluate whether directions are clear and attainable, design unique graphic organizers, and are creative in their approach to the learning process. ELL teachers understand where there are gaps in understanding and bridge those gaps regardless of language differences. ELL teachers instinctively know when a task is an insurmountable mountain and which skill is the most useful to extract from that mountain.

Use the co-teachers. It cannot be overstated what a great asset they are in the classroom. Does this mean planning together? Yes. Giving up some control in your classroom? Yes. Understanding there is another expert in the room beyond yourself? Yes. Will the outcome be more than you imagined? Speaking from experience with deep collaboration with our co-teachers, absolutely yes.

Technology

Nothing can fully replace the valuable face-to-face conversation we would love to have with every student as much as possible; however, there are digital tools at our disposal that can offer alternatives to protect our class time. In future chapters, we discuss how to use videoconferencing as a means of moving the conversation outside the classroom. Additionally, we discuss audio-recording feedback that simulates a conversation and has the potential to offer more personalized feedback to students.

While these tools do not fully replace the one-on-one conference, they offer many of the same benefits of conferencing: a sense of personalized attention, individualized feedback, and intimate work around writing in a digitally created space of conversation. Using these tools at targeted times with strategically chosen students can assist teachers in conferencing with more students and protect instructional time.

Class Leaders

We all know the students in class who have the respect of their peers. Whether these students are high skilled or simply charismatic (or both), they can be a valuable asset to utilize when teacher attention is focused on one student in a conference. These students could help answer basic questions, direct students to needed resources, help with the distribution of materials, or even offer advice to other students if appropriate or relevant. Leveraging these young leaders (especially if a co-teacher is not an option) can fortify a conference against interruptions and foster a classroom culture with greater student ownership and buy-in.

Varied Lesson Structures

In later chapters, we delineate lesson options that can offer structures to help with conferencing in the secondary classroom and a large student body. In addition to technological tools, small group instruction or "stations" lessons can offer more personalized conversation for a few students at a time. In the chapters on brainstorming (chapter 3) and revision (chapter 5), we discuss how to focus on small groups of students based on specific student needs, skill deficiencies, similar challenges, or targeted writing practices. These small-group conversations (described in detail later) afford the benefit of allowing teachers to see a few students at one time and still provide students with a more intimate space to ask questions, request advice, or share challenges.

WHAT ARE THE OTHER STUDENTS DOING?

Clear Expectations

A meaningful conversation between a student and teacher cannot happen if the teacher must spend time redirecting the class. Every time the instructor looks up to tell the class to quiet down or to focus or to remind them the class work will be collected is a break in the conversational flow of the conference. Imagine trying to have a conversation with someone who gets up every minute to do something else. In essence, that is what a teacher does when he or she has to stop for classroom management.

Creating a culture where all members treat conferences as sacrosanct goes a long way toward limiting the amount of classroom management a teacher must do. The other part of this is providing tasks that are authentic and not just busy work for students to complete. Could students complete work for the next unit? Are the students engaged in another stage of the writing process?

Establish the task the students must accomplish in the class period. The students who are working independently need the following:

- An explanation of the task
- A checklist of items to complete or elements necessary in the writing
- An end-of-period expectation
- A timer for time management

Teachers want students to be independent or moving toward independence. Every student leaves high school for college, vocational training, or a job. In each of those scenarios, young adults have to manage their time based on the expectations of others while advocating for themselves. The conferencing classroom reinforces these skills.

The real question that often makes the task of conferencing seem too insurmountable to tackle: how do we keep the rest of the class engaged while our attention is focused on one student? As discussed in other parts of this book, culture is crucial. Developing and fostering buy-in for conferences takes time and effort, but both are well spent if the outcome allows for meaningful conversations with students to encourage their voice as writers and autonomy over their own academic progress.

General Options and Critical Attributes: Meaningful, High-Stakes, Graded Assignments

In other chapters, we consider specific tasks that students could focus on during conferences at different points in the writing process. In these chapters, we also give detailed examples to illuminate what these tasks look like in the classroom. The choices teachers make for these assignments are largely dependent on classroom contexts of grade, student population, curriculum demands, and course focus. Broadly speaking, there are several options, including short writing or reading tasks, prepping for the conference, timed writing, multiple-choice or short-answer assessments, independent reading, surveys, and peer- or self-editing assignments.

Whatever students are working on concurrently with conferencing, it must be meaningful, high-stakes, and graded work. If students sense they are laden with "busy work" during this time, focus will quickly wane and our conference time will unravel as we attempt to both manage a class and have an individual conversation. Assignments must be clearly tied to course objectives, standards, and work that students recognize as improving skills they seek to improve.

Teachers should avoid a large pile of grading as a result of conference time, but it is crucial that students understand the work has value and should generally be attached to a grade. Completion grades are not generally meaningful, but there are times they may be appropriate or necessary given an English teacher's grading load. Peer editing, quick writes, or other low-stakes assessments are options that keep grading manageable but still show students their work is important.

Vocabulary quizzes, short reading responses, or other independent work that can be quickly monitored, assessed, and recorded are also options that keep students focused and open up time and space for conferencing. As much as possible, giving students grades quickly—even as conferences are going on—demonstrates to students that this time should be utilized to its fullest and that the work submitted at the end of class (not after!) has visible consequences and an effect on their performance in the class as a whole.

Specific Assignments for Different Phases of the Writing Process

Many of the assignments suggested here are discussed in more detail in future chapters. Broadly, each stage of the writing process affords different options for students' focus while conferences are running concurrently. During the brainstorming and outlining stage, students could be searching for evidence, continuing their own outline, conferring or evaluating peers' evidence or outlines, or beginning the writing task (for higher-skilled students). In the drafting and revision stages, most students are already in the process of writing or revising, so quick one-on-one conversations can happen in the midst of this work. Incremental deadlines at these phases can also keep the class on track during conferences. Additionally, focused and specific peer-editing assignments or self-reflective editing assignments are productive options to open windows for conferencing time. Please see future chapters for more detailed descriptions and example assignments.

Task Sheets

Ms. Patterson designs task sheets in a way that promotes student self-direction. On the top, she provides the objectives followed by a list that students check off as they complete the different components. The checklist also enables the teacher to walk around and monitor student progress between conferences.

Students must work toward an objective. If the class is working on introductions, the conference will be with students who might have difficulty with this task while the rest of the class is writing a thesis statement and introduction on their own. The checklist might include the components of the introduction, including a final step of a peer review and feedback (a small note really). The day's final item might be a revision based on feedback.

Students also benefit from a column that tracks accomplishments, questions, and struggles. The student at the end of class completes the following sentence stems:

- I feel confident about . . .
- I have questions about . . .
- I am struggling with . . .

The completed sentence stems become a starting point for conversation with the instructor later.

A timer is a simple addition, but it cannot be overstated how much students need to see the amount of time provided for a task. Adults take for granted the internal clock that ticks within us to help manage time. Everyone can develop this skill over time, but students benefit from external management tools.

Assignments Using Technology

Students will not be writing every time a teacher conducts a conference. Beyond packets and readings, consider using Screencastify, which is a Google add-on. This app allows the teacher to capture activity on the computer screen while providing narration. Mrs. Abraham uses the app primarily to teach mini-lessons on citations, how to introduce data, and quotes when in the research paper unit. These videos are housed on the Google Drive attached to the class Stream in Google Classroom. And best of all, the videos may be used throughout the school year and in later years.

Need to review a skill? Use Edpuzzle to post review videos and attached questions. You may assign Castle Learning assignments for grammar, punctuation, and reading lessons. For example, Castle Learning has 334 questions related to Edgar Allan Poe to mix and match to a particular story or poem. Newsela is a website that presents articles at varying reading levels for students. Create a class, add students, assign an article, and have students answer multiple-choice questions and short-answer prompts.

Again, little of this is possible without a culture of respect. Students respect the time allotted to the student in conference by not engaging in off-task behavior, and the teacher respects students outside the conference by assigning authentic learning tasks. Do not hesitate to tell students why the task is assigned, what skills are being taught or reinforced, or what component of a later larger task the current assignment is part of.

HOW DO I MONITOR THE REST OF THE CLASS?

A low-tech way to monitor the class is simply to get up between conferences and walk around. In an effort to save time, it might appear to be easier just to go on to the next student. But not walking around periodically means wasting time in the middle of a conference to tell the class to refocus.

For group work, consider a rubric on the desk. This is a simple solution. The math teachers at East-West (our school) created a rubric with a range from 1 to 4 assessing group function. The laminated rubric is taped on the group desk, and the teachers use a dry erase marker. If a group is doing poorly, they are told the teacher will return to reassess and give a better grade if it warrants. The ELL teacher Mr. Jacobson revised the protocol for English (see fig. 2.4).

For technology-based classrooms, Ms. Santos prefers students to write using Google Docs in the classroom. This means that at any time she can enter into a student's shared document to assess writing or task progress. At the beginning of the school year, Ms. Santos asks the students to create

Figure 2.4. **Group Rubric**

4	We're Going Above and Beyond
We are considering the specific needs of our group.
We are all contributing insightful and unique ideas.
We ask each other questions to deepen understanding.
3	We're Good
We know our roles.
We are all engaged and participating based on the assigned role.
We are on track to finish the task.
We ask each other questions to deepen understanding.
2	We're Stuck
We have a question that we can't answer.
We are stuck on the next steps—what do we do now?
One or some of the group hasn't spoken or participated.
We have asked some but not enough questions.
1	We're Not Productive
We don't know what to do.
We are disruptive or are having a conflict.
We haven't decided on roles or haven't started the task.
We are not asking questions.

a folder in their Google Drive labeled with their name and class period. As each student shares their folder, she moves the folder into a larger folder titled with the class period and school year. From that point, students are instructed to keep every document they create in the class in that specific folder. This means that students no longer need to share each file with the teacher.

Ms. Santos monitors progress or lack thereof while also engaging in conversation with students. It only takes moments to recognize a nonconferencing student is off task and pop into a student file as an icon in the corner. It's even worse when the icon starts a chat. Ms. Santos does not have to speak over the class and disrupt the other students, nor does she cause any public embarrassment for the student by calling out poor behavior.

The Stream feature in Google Classroom can also be a way for students to ask questions in a nonvocal manner when the instructor is involved in conferencing. Use the smart board to project the class Stream, and students may type in questions or issues they want addressed. This does mean that between conversations the teacher must check the Stream.

Middle school students are less independent and benefit from reward-based management. ClassDojo is a tool middle school English and language arts teachers can use during conferences; the teacher can have students listed on the board (as a screen in ClassDojo) as a way to monitor and demonstrate attention to the rest of the class even if it is divided. The teacher can assign a rotating job of ClassDojo monitor to award points for positive behavior. If students are displayed on a smart board screen, the teacher can quickly give rewards (or penalties) for their focus while they are not in a conference.

Students may also turn in reflections from their daily work that provide data about what they accomplished and what they struggled with during that period or task. Any issues could be addressed in the next class before conferences progress if you have consecutive days of conferencing.

HOW DO I MEASURE SUCCESS WHEN STUDENTS DO NOT BUY IN?

Every conversation will not be a profound moment of understanding for the student. To expect this is to invite acute disappointment. There will be students who find conferences a waste of time. Why talk when they could just read feedback and make changes? Others might balk at being grouped together for conversations. Having someone else know about a weakness seems too vulnerable.

When teachers track conversations over the school year, it is easier to note the small advances a student makes. Perhaps the first time, the students had short responses to questions and did not ask any questions of the teacher. Maybe next time, there was a question asked. And another time, a dynamic back-and-forth developed as the student pushed back on suggestions or asked for clarification.

Do not give up on the student who hates to have these types of conversations. It is okay to have short, seemingly unproductive conversations. It will not be that way all year. Any progress is progress, and all students will move at their own pace depending on their need. Just meet them where they are right now.

SUMMARY

Conferences are manageable when

- Classroom structures are created that reinforce expectations and agreed-upon protocols
- The physical arrangement of the classroom is conducive to a private conversation with the teacher and classroom management
- There is an understanding that conferences may look different at various stages of the writing process
- Other resources such as co-teachers are part of conferencing to see more students
- Opportunities exist for reflection throughout the school year

- Teachers assign authentic assignments for students not in conference; this may take various forms with the help of student-friendly applications and websites along with traditional no-tech assignments
- Systems are in place to organize hard copies of writing or online portfolios
- Teachers accept that occasionally the success arrives in small doses and looks different for every student

Part II

Tools and Examples for Specific Types of Conferences

THREE
Before Writing
Brainstorming and Outlining

Anthony Liu walks into second period the way he always does: trudging, eyes downcast, grumbling under his breath. I can almost see the Charlie Brown cloud following above his path. This kid is aggravating me. He's always so negative—what's his problem?

In our conference I find out: he's frustrated. He doesn't understand the assignment and feels unconfident as a writer. Our conversation changes my whole perception of him. I now recognize that the behavior I interpreted as trivial teenage angst is actually more complicated. Without the opportunity to speak with him, I may never have understood or been able to assist him as effectively. — Amy

Student conferences are valuable because they provide an opportunity for tailored feedback and a meaningful impact on student writing. Further, they foster greater ownership and agency for students and their own learning.

With this in mind, the benefits of conferencing can begin at the initial stages of the writing process during brainstorming and outlining. Meeting with students at this point can be particularly valuable for checking for comprehension, staving off misunderstandings, and eventually producing a higher-quality work product.

A student conference before writing might seem premature, and for some students, it is. Those are the students who thrive in the brainstorming stage and who can formulate an overarching plan for their writing, some regardless of whether they can accomplish their set objective completely. Additionally, conversations with targeted students at this point (and at other points) in the writing process allow for differentiation and purposeful instruction based on student needs.

Students who benefit from conferences at this stage in particular are those who struggle with comprehension and breaking down and prioritizing parts of a larger writing tasks. Students who need support evaluating evidence, organizing reasons, or sequencing for cohesion are ideal candidates for these early conferences. For the majority of students, a conference before writing stimulates thought and eases anxiety about the writing assignment.

With these purposes and benefits in mind, this chapter provides tools, strategies, and examples to help students and teachers plan and prepare for productive brainstorming and outlining conferences, along with later midpoint check-ins.

EXAMPLES AND PRACTICES FOR BRAINSTORMING CONFERENCES

Conferencing before students begin to plan and outline is a form of equity. Students who do not understand the prompt are at a disadvantage even before they determine their thesis or look for textual evidence. Only a small group of students in the classroom will need assistance articulating in their own words the demands of the prompt and their plan for their writing.

The thrill of a new writing prompt is perhaps a source of excitement only for the teacher assigning the topic and a few students who enjoy writing. But for some students, the first obstacle is not the planning and outlining but rather just comprehending *what the prompt is asking*. Making time to meet with specific students before they begin outlining may prevent later pitfalls. In every class, there are only a few students who need conferencing at this stage.

Even before meeting with students, teachers must determine who needs additional assistance. Essay topics assigned at the end of class are not a good idea. Present the topic with enough time for students to process the assignment and for you to correct misconceptions or provide assistance. A period spent breaking down the prompt, conferencing with needier students, and providing opportunities for other students to start their work is an investment in a stronger product.

While teachers need not conference with all or even a third of the class at this stage, it is still daunting to determine who needs that one-on-one conversation. After reading the prompt together, provide all students with index cards. Writing on index cards is less intimidating, particularly for student writers who find the broad expanse of paper a mental Mount Everest. Give students time to answer the questions below. It makes sense to have students focus, on the first day, on the first three questions.

The others should be saved for another day, or used as next steps for students who understand the prompt well already and want to move forward on the first day.

Potential questions for a brainstorming conference:

- What does the prompt ask you to do?
- What type of writing is this?
- What type of support or examples do you need to fully develop an answer to the prompt?
- Where will you find relevant evidence?
- What is one specific example you can use now?

Before We Climb Everest: Using Brief Responses to Determine Early Needs

As students quietly answer the above brainstorming questions, the teacher collects data. Who seems to be struggling to answer the first three questions? Whose answers seem a few steps removed in understanding from their peers?

At this point, there are multiple options.

First, the teacher can identify who needs further assistance and gather a group of students to conference with using the questions above as a guide. A group no larger than five but no smaller than two provides a space to ask questions and to clarify misunderstandings without the stigma of a one-on-one conversation that screams "I (me only me!) need help." In regard to classroom management, the last three questions are what keep the rest of the students engaged while the teacher conducts the mini-conferences.

The second option is for students to partner with an elbow mate or create groups and exchange answers to questions one to three. In a turn-and-talk, every student has to engage in a mini-conference. Turn-and-talks work best when there is an established culture of directed peer-to-peer conversation. The teacher can also visit small groups of students for conversations. It is not, however, difficult to create that community, since it is just a matter of providing students an opportunity to speak to each other before presenting their responses to the whole class. This is particularly helpful for English language learner (ELL) students who prefer to ask questions to peers in their dominant or home language.

A final option is to collect the index cards, read over the answers, and engage in conferences in the next class while the other students are planning and outlining. The conversations need not be long. The conversation revolves around questions already asked of the students. Some students need the back-and-forth of a verbal exchange to be able to articulate and refine their own questions about the prompt.

Regardless of which option is pursued, the index cards should be collected for a review.

Teacher Reflection

Index cards are great for a quick perusal of student understanding before having any conversation one-on-one. Students who have similar misunderstandings may be grouped together during the conference in an effort to save time. The group conversation is more effective because students find the answers for questions they did not know they needed to ask. —Ms. Anderson

Elevator Pitch: Quick Conversations to Test Ideas

Another way to assess a student's understanding of the prompt is the "elevator pitch," which is a short verbal expression of an idea. Invite students to complete an elevator pitch for their writing. In thirty seconds to one minute, the student should indicate the following:

- Essay topic
- Overall thesis direction
- One example they will use

The elevator pitch could be made to the teacher or to multiple peers in a speed-dating-type presentation. A pitch to the teacher means that even the teacher provides feedback using the one-minute time constraint. At this stage, the teacher is only assessing whether the students *understand* the prompt and if the student has a direction and has found valid textual support. In this scenario, the students come to the teacher one-on-one. The addition of a probing question might generate new student ideas without overwhelming them with too much feedback.

For the speed-dating-type elevator pitch, have the students create two sets of parallel lines with students facing each other. The students present their answers to the questions above and then take turns being the person making the pitch and the student providing feedback. The teacher is the data collector in this exercise, noting who has the most difficulty expressing their plans. The students should get a chance to speak to five people.

Students might figure out which of their peers has similar ideas and which provide actionable feedback, which could be helpful later when they are stuck or doing peer editing. It is best to model the speed-dating version of the pitch with the teacher and student role-playing. Students are not going to remember all their feedback. As one of the parallel lines moves seat to seat, they travel with a "note catcher." Before each student makes the pitch to the other, they exchange the note catcher for the listener to write notes on.

After everyone has seen hopefully five but at least three people, allow time for quiet written reflection, listing next steps or making the changes advised. During reflection time, the teacher should pull out the students who seemed to be most confused.

Teacher Reflection

The speed-dating exercise is a loud exercise. Even though I was prepared for an elevated noise level, I was not prepared. I should have normed for voice levels prior to the activity. When one pair is speaking with an outside voice, so are the pairs on either side. Timers for the rounds are vital, as some pairs speak too little and some want to speak more. In addition, allow time for setting up and breaking down the seats. —Mr. Gruet

Commit to a Topic: Narrowing the Focus of Research Papers

The above breakdown of the essay prompt works when all the students have the same prompt. This is not always the case. For research papers or topics in which students self-select, it may be useful to conference with students at another point. For example, when students select their own topic for a research paper, there are two junctures (research question development and thesis formulation) at which to conference with students prior to outlining or writing.

Figure 3.1. Speed-dating picture Photo by Amy Matthusen

For example, the tenth graders in Mr. Gruet's class have a self-selected argumentative research paper that is followed by a TED Talk–type presentation about an aspect of their issue. A research paper is only as strong as the initial research question. Not all student interests make for the best topics, so Mr. Gruet devotes time in class for students to pinpoint their focus. The tenth graders were given a sheet on which they listed not only their interests but also social issues they were angry or passionate about.

For a week before students honed their research topic, their homework was to watch or read the news from sources Mr. Gruet selected. The interest aspect is more involved than it appears because most students tend to say they do not have any interests. For others, the interest was electronics centered. So some students were further prompted to think about what they enjoyed doing or what they liked to read about even though most other times they hated to read.

From that point, the students select the one topic they would not mind researching more, identify controversial/arguable aspects about that topic, and settle on a research question. At this point, students exchange papers with a peer, who provides feedback on the research question. The student then applies the feedback to create a stronger research question. The collected sheets are examined by Mr. Gruet. The next day, when other students are moving on to the next step (creating a list of questions needed to be answered to be experts on their topic of research), Mr. Gruet conferences with the students whose revised questions were weak.

These conferences are only with students who are stuck, who have impossible topics, or who are lost. The conversation between the student and Mr. Gruet only lasts three to five minutes and often less. The first option is to assist the student in revising the research question. If that is a dead end, the teacher goes back to the original list and asks probing questions.

A tenth grader named Kayla was stuck. For most papers, Kayla takes time to figure out what she wants to write and waits to ask for help. In addition, Kayla has difficulty articulating the kind of help she needs. Since Mr. Gruet collected the index cards before, he knew Kayla was not clear about her research paper topic. Mr. Gruet made a list of students he wanted to call for a brief meeting, and Kayla was at the top of the list.

MR. GRUET: Do you have any other interests that you didn't write down?
KAYLA: No.
MR. GRUET: What do you like to do?
KAYLA: I don't know.
MR. GRUET: I see you put down conspiracy theories.
KAYLA: Yeah. I watch a lot about that.
MR. GRUET: Anything specific?
KAYLA: No. Everything.

MR. GRUET: Like aliens?
KAYLA: No. The DNA tests.
MR. GRUET: What about them?
KAYLA: What the companies do. They keep the DNA.
MR. GRUET: So, about privacy?
KAYLA: Yeah and what they do with the DNA.

After a few more questions, Kayla was able to decide to write about whether there should be regulations regarding genealogy test results. The back-and-forth forced her to articulate what she was unable to do before since she did not know what questions to ask herself.

Teacher Reflection

The whole class does not need this conversation. Triage the needs. Speak to those who are the most lost so the rest of the class is not held back by a whole-class lesson on topic revision. These conferences are short, always less than five minutes, and while the rest of the class is moving forward. The conference at this stage is vital because the student can work through the problems before they become too intimidated by the progress their peers are making and which they are not making. —Mr. Gruet

Online Discussion: Using Technology to Share Initial Thoughts

Below is not a conference but an idea on how to save time when scheduling does not allow for conferences at the topic selection stage. The use of technology speeds up the process and engages all students as they discuss and receive feedback online.

Having conferences and conversations early in the writing process helps sharpen focus to arrive at a clear stance before embarking on the journey of writing. Online discussions are not conferences per se, but they are an option that offer many of the same benefits. These early messy or overarching discussions can often coalesce or distill different thoughts into a stronger thesis or assertion to guide writing. Additionally, these forums allow for testing ideas, sharing perspectives, and considering possibilities that might eventually become supporting points of body paragraphs.

Another alternative to the time and logistical demands of individual conferences at this stage is to move these conversations to an online venue. Google Classroom "questions," Blackboard, Turnitin, and other online resources offer spaces for teachers and students to participate and engage in these debates outside of instructional time. Moreover, these spaces can offer many of the same benefits in the exchange of ideas that ultimately serve to hone and refine students' thoughts before writing.

In an eleventh grade AP language class, students read articles and debated the benefits and drawbacks of instituting a national language. After considering different perspectives, students turned to the overall essay prompt: Should English be America's national language? The following excerpts from the online discussion are by Chris and Paulina, both juniors and ELL students.

> *Chris:* English should be America's national language because it helps to unify Americans. Even though America is composed of various cultures and people, English is the most common language in America. American society already encourages people to know how to speak English. Without knowing how to speak English, people will find difficulty in participating in social activities because most things are written in English. As an immigrant, I experienced that it is hard to live daily life without knowing how to speak English. Even in school, I was encouraged to learn English because everything is written and spoken in English. If I refused to learn English then I would fall behind.

> *Paulina:* English should not be America's national language because America is a nation of immigrants. It will be hard for people to conform and learn the English language. English is not the only language being spoken in America. There are many other languages being spoken, for example: Spanish, Chinese, French, Korean, Tagalog, Vietnamese, etc. What will happen to them if English was to be the national language? . . . America does not need a national language to unite as a whole, other criteria that the nation shares keeps us together, like having respect for individuals and opportunity for all. We started off without a national language, why should we need a national language now? Therefore English is not needed to be America's national language.

Going online for the discussion was a nice way to give us different perspectives on the issue. We got to see what the class was thinking, including some students who don't talk in class. It helped me think about what to do for my counterargument. —Paulina

✍ Teacher Reflection

It's interesting that Chris and Paulina are using similar reasoning; viewing each other's stance and reasoning can provide an opportunity for each student to refine his or her thinking before tackling the larger assignment. Both Paulina and Chris can now begin writing with a clearer understanding of the debate and their own stances within it. Students could also quote each other's online posts as a way to address a counterargument. Another option is to select a few students' postings to use in a gallery walk and then extend the debate into class discussion before writing. With any structure, this allows an alternative to conferences during class time with many of the same essential benefits. —Ms. Dylan

EXAMPLES AND PRACTICES FOR OUTLINING CONFERENCES

It's worth remembering here (and at other points of this book) that teachers will likely run up against their limits of class time (and personal sanity) if they try to see every student at every point of the writing process. With this in mind, targeting students at different stages helps make conversations manageable and purposeful. Having conferences at the outlining stage can help focus attention on students who may need extra help evaluating evidence, sequencing ideas for cohesion, and checking for strong connections.

Clearly, there are many ways to outline. While some students prefer categories of the classic outline, others are more comfortable with bullet points or a version of a text-heavy mind map. Students should be encouraged to use any style that helps them organize their thoughts in a meaningful way. Before conferencing, teachers can model different outline structures and strategies to help make this choice informed and meaningful for student use.

Conferences at the outlining stage provide permission to organize in the most compatible manner in order to elicit the best representation of a student's plan. Once the outlines are complete, collect them. It is tempting to provide a quick completion grade for this assignment. Avoid this temptation. Make the outline a grade and evaluate the same skills you hope to improve with students (quality of examples, cohesion, connections). It is easier to redirect a student in the outline phase than when they have a rough draft they are attached to and less inclined to change dramatically.

Potential questions for outlining conferences:

- Explain the assignment in your own words.
- Talk through your outline: what is your rationale for the examples you chose?
- How does each example connect to your thesis?
- How did you decide the order of examples?
- Explain one example in detail and talk through how you will use it in your paper.
- Ask one question you would like answered or one piece of advice you would like for this assignment.

Talk Me through It: Classic Outline Conference

In an eleventh grade AP language class, students develop a position on the claim of whether or not checking social network profiles is an acceptable practice for potential employers or college admissions officers. While other students are completing a multiple-choice practice session, a few students step out for a quick conference on the outlines they're working on. Ms. Dylan sits right outside the classroom with a view of the other students, but with enough space to have a private conversation.

PATTY: So I'm going to say that colleges and businesses should not look at applicants' social network pages. Those are personal. They aren't part of what colleges should care about. I think I will use the source that says students feel checking social networks is wrong for colleges to do. Most students agree it shouldn't be used.

MS. DYLAN: Could you explain that reason a little more?

PATTY: Sure. Students don't want colleges looking at their social media accounts. That is their social life. Not their academic or school life. So it shouldn't matter because it has nothing to do with who they are as students.

MS. DYLAN: Okay. So why do you think colleges might want to view that information?

PATTY: Well, I think maybe they want to learn more about who's applying. Who they are.

MS. DYLAN: Tell me more about that.

PATTY: It might help them get to know someone more. But I still think it's not really their business. That's private.

MS. DYLAN: You're making some points that you can definitely use for a persuasive essay. Let's take it a little further and consider a couple ideas: (1) Colleges and employers can only see what is already public. It may still be an ethical invasion of privacy, but the information itself is still public. (2) Students may not like colleges viewing their profiles. But you also suggested that it's a way to "get to know someone more." If colleges want to get to know their applicants more (as you say), why shouldn't they look at social network information? Just answering this kind of question already takes your reasoning further and makes it more complex. To construct a really persuasive position, consider how you would convince someone who you respect, but with whom you also disagree.

Teacher Reflection

I wish I had asked Patty more questions to lead her thought process rather than establish a line of reasoning for her at the end of this conversation.

Nevertheless, I think our talk will help Patty refine her thinking and reasoning before writing. Without this conference, her writing would probably not have the same level of thought or detail. —Ms. Dylan

Think outside the Classroom: Video-Recording Outline Conferences

Sometimes it's a benefit when conversations happen outside of class, saving instructional time and averting potential management challenges. Listening or responding to videos generally doesn't take long, and there is still the sense of a one-on-one conversation and individualized feedback.

Some students are not comfortable recording themselves; if this is an option you're considering using frequently, early conversations establishing trust and the purpose of recordings are helpful. Some students could use the platform just to record the audio, while keeping the camera on something other than their face. They may also be assuaged if you tell them you will be the only person viewing the video (which is an option in the settings). Finally, sharing a model of your own or a student's video can alleviate some of the concerns students may face if they see that the example isn't perfect. Establishing a culture early on where vulnerabilities are encouraged and all students feel willing and encouraged to contribute will help make this practice more tenable.

Donata is in Mr. Alvarez's eleventh grade American literature class with mixed-level students, several of whom are ELL. The essay assignment asked students to select one of three shorter responses to literary criticism connected to *The Great Gatsby*, then expand shorter response into an essay. The assignment asked students to record a video using Flipgrid, explaining the assignment in their own words, then to discuss an example they were thinking of using, and finally to ask a question (or request advice) for any aspect of the assignment.

> *Donata:* For my essay I'm going to talk about Strba [a feminist reading] and *The Great Gatsby*. So in Strba's article he talks about how all the women's power and wealth [is] originated from men. And in *The Great Gatsby*'s novel, to an extent it explains and supports that.
>
> One evidence that I'll be using is from page 133, said by Daisy, she says, "I did love him once, but I love you *too*." This connects to the idea of women relying on men because she—I believe that she is conflicting between Tom and Gatsby mainly because she doesn't know if she wants to give up the state that she's in being with Tom as his wife. Because being his wife, she has less problems. She doesn't have to worry about her parents or her friends. And the fact that she has a child now.
>
> But if she leaves with Gatsby, she has to worry [about that]. I believe she would encounter some type of conflict. And there's going to

be some consequences. So she tells the two men that she doesn't know who she really loves.

So then one question I had was I do not know how to conclude the three women, which is Myrtle, Daisy, and Jordan [as examples in the essay]. I don't know how I should connect them.

Ms. Alvarez: Thanks for your video. I thought you had a really nice quote from chapter 7 when Daisy says, "I loved you too." I like what you were saying about it and how you recognized Daisy's internal conflict when she is torn between Gatsby and Tom for good reasons. Remember Strba also says that Daisy is not her own *person*. So think a little about what you were saying about Daisy: she is torn between Tom and Gatsby. Now bring that back a little more to Strba's interpretation of Daisy: *does* she have a character of her own? Is she at all her own person? Is she only defined by these relationships with men? It sounds like you're thinking about this already, just make the connection a little clearer when you start writing.

Your other question was about how to conclude the essay. I have a couple ideas for you. At the end of the article, Strba suggests that Gatsby's women characters show that Fitzgerald was not entirely comfortable with women starting to gain more independence at this time in history. That's one possibility: think about where the novel fits historically, perhaps drawing from your U.S. history class.

The other idea that could be interesting to write about in conclusion is to consider: are the women characters in Gatsby really mostly negative [as Strba suggests]? Or is there any aspect of them that makes them more sympathetic? I'd be really curious to hear what you think about that after writing about Myrtle, Daisy, and Jordan, and it could be a way to draw them together in a conclusion. Let me know in class if I can help at all as you're writing and see you soon!

Tips and Ideas for Using Flipgrid

- Set time limits for video recordings to keep conversations/videos focused and concise.
- Adjust the settings on Flipgrid so that only you and the student view each other's videos (this may set some students' concerns at ease).
- For ELL students, this can offer valuable practice speaking.
- Try a practice run with a few students first to troubleshoot any technological glitches before rolling out to a whole class (or classes).
- Small tips: Students cannot see instructor video feedback on the app; they must go to the website my.flipgrid.com. For individualized video responses to students, instructors should not "reply" to videos but should instead select "add private video feedback."

> Video-recording conferences on platforms like Flipgrid is an alternative to the classroom conference.

What I liked about Flipgrid is it's more of a conversation than emailing the problems that we have. I can hear your feedback more easily and take a better understanding of what you're implying. — Tiffany

 Teacher Reflection

I think this conference was really helpful for both Donata and me. Donata should have more cohesion and connections in her writing with this feedback. It also helps me hone my instruction: now I can consider covering conclusions for the class as a whole. Overall, this conversation highlights a few aspects that demonstrate the benefits of an early conference for both student and teacher. — Ms. Alvarez

WHAT ARE OTHER STUDENTS DOING?

At this point in the writing process, students not involved in conferences could work on a variety of tasks: prepping for their conference (if applicable), continuing their own outline, conferring or evaluating peers' outlines, beginning the writing task, or completing other possible short reading or writing tasks. Alternatively, teachers could ask students to take part in a more formal assignment, such as "Pitch It to a Peer," to get early feedback on their brainstorming and outlining.

Pitch It to a Peer

If the writing is taking place in class, students are probably at a variety of stages as they brainstorm and outline. Since most classes have a range of skill levels and backgrounds, you could consider possibilities for different levels of students.

High-skilled students may be able to segue directly into the writing process. They could also take part in "Pitch It to a Peer" or potentially act as a resource to struggling students. These students may also be up for an additional challenge with the writing assignment, fleshing out a new idea, writing technique, or structure that the rest of the class may not be ready for.

Students that struggle to get started or need help fleshing out their writing plan may need this time to continue work on their outlines. These students will also likely be the focus of these early conferences but could also participate in a "Pitch It to a Peer" conference.

For the many students who fall in between these ranges, teachers could ask them to pitch their outlines to a peer. This allows students to hone ideas and get early feedback. If it makes sense for the writing process, have students construct their outlines in the form of a slide presentation. Students could then "pitch" their outlines constructed as slides (PowerPoint or Google Slides) and lead the listener through their initial plans as a mini-presentation. The listener/student could take notes along a simple guideline: note three positive aspects of the outline, pose three questions to the writer, offer three ideas to consider as the writer moves forward. After offering this feedback, they could then switch roles.

SUMMARY

Brainstorming conferences are beneficial because they

- Help avert early misunderstandings that would only be exacerbated later in the writing process
- Test the clarity of our initial instruction
- Address minor issues before they become major problems
- Have the potential to lead to higher-quality, more nuanced writing products

Outlining conferences are beneficial because they

- Allow for revision of subtopics and organization before writing
- Troubleshoot potential issues before pen meets paper (or fingers meet keyboard)

Students who benefit from conferences at these stages are

- ELL students who may have misunderstood the text or task
- Writers who struggle to break big tasks down into more manageable chunks
- Writers who have trouble getting started, but often prevail after the initial hump
- Writers who like to verbalize initial ideas before formalizing them in writing

Effective conferences at this stage

- Check for students' understanding of their writing task
- Help students articulate a plan for writing
- Give students clear next steps
- Help students evaluate examples for relevance and cohesion before writing
- Put the onus of preparation (as always) on the student rather than the teacher
- Allow for targeted and honed instruction afterward

FOUR
During Writing
Drafting Conferences

By looking through my work in a conference, I was able to see trends and figure out my own progress. —Ritu, high school senior

As long as both the student and teacher are comfortable, the conference will likely be successful. A conversation cannot be led by a nervous student who is uncomfortable talking to a teacher; little information will be revealed and whatever thoughts and ideas the student wants to reveal to the teacher during the conversation may also likely be suppressed. Therefore, it is highly recommended, to any teacher, that in order to lead a successful conference, a successful teacher–student relationship must be established (to the point where a student can even go to the teacher outside of classes with ease). —Serdo, high school senior

[Conferences go well] when the teacher is open-minded and attentive, while the student is honest. If a student denies their own faults and weaknesses, there is no way it can proceed smoothly or work because the teacher would be forced to assign them a grade without their cooperation. In addition, if the student is too passive, they are just not showing off what they can do and it reduces grading accuracy. —Pamela, high school senior

Teachers often do not conference with students at the drafting stage of writing, but there can be distinct benefits to speaking with students at this stage. As Ritu suggested in her conference, stepping back from a piece of writing to catch common or repeated mistakes or acknowledge progress is important for improving writing, building confidence, and working through feedback and next steps. Some groups of students benefit, in particular, from conferences at this stage.

For students who get stuck, this can help them get over a hump. Students writing on a text but who were not able to complete the entire book may be able to start a writing task, but they may stall midway through the writing process. For these students, a check-in conference can increase their chances of seeing the assignment through to completion. Any student who struggles with deadlines is a natural focus for a conference during drafting. For these students (and others), this type of conference keeps the writing in motion—a crucial nudge that propels when they might otherwise stagnate.

EXAMPLES AND PRACTICES FOR DRAFTING CONFERENCES

This chapter offers ideas and practices for conferencing with students during the drafting stage of writing. In particular, these conversations highlight the *process* of writing over the *product*, to make the moves writers make visible to students both in actual writing and in follow-up conversations. Even brief conversations at this stage can help students overcome frustration, understand confusing points, and appreciate that no matter what a writer's skill level, the undertaking can be messy, disorganized, and daunting at times. Sharing vulnerabilities and frustrations through this point can eventually become empowering if these challenges are shared and met with suggestions for next steps.

Questions for drafting conferences:

- How far are you in the drafting process?
- Are there any challenges or points you are stuck on?
- How are you using the grading criteria or models as you write?
- Do you have a plan for moving forward?

Set the Stage: Sloppy Collective Writing for Follow-up Drafting Conferences

Chapter 1 discussed the importance of building classroom culture to aid in student conferences. This work is often accomplished when teachers share their own vulnerabilities as writers and make them explicit for students. These weaknesses can easily be displayed during the *process* of writing. Our inclination as teachers is to share model products to guide students as they write. Students may be better served, however, by seeing more of the imperfect and messy drafting that happens (for all of us) before arriving at a more polished piece.

One way to expose students to this process is to write a collective sloppy paragraph together as a class. Work on a prompt or portion of an assignment that is similar to an upcoming task. Have students transcribe the paragraph as you write it together. This transcription can serve as a model to reference later. Start with the topic sentence and continue sentence by sentence or even phrase by phrase through the paragraph. Talk through the choices made and how they relate to the task. Ask students for suggestions as you write. Most importantly, make mistakes. Lots of them. Cross words out. Rewrite. Add a transition. Rework the structure of the sentence. Change diction and phrasing. Show students the messiness of writing as the paragraph forms in a way that makes the process visible.

After finishing the paragraph, ask students: Was this helpful? What questions does writing this paragraph raise? What are your takeaways for your own writing? Even brief, bulleted responses to these questions on index cards can become the basis of later conversations and conferences and encourage metacognitive skills. As students continue writing from this point, teachers could circulate and read responses on index cards (or if collected, know with whom they should follow up the next day). Especially if the practice raises questions for certain students, getting to them first for a quick conference could offer valuable feedback to help the student produce a stronger piece of writing.

Writing the paragraph together gave me a better idea of what to do with my own essay. — Angelica

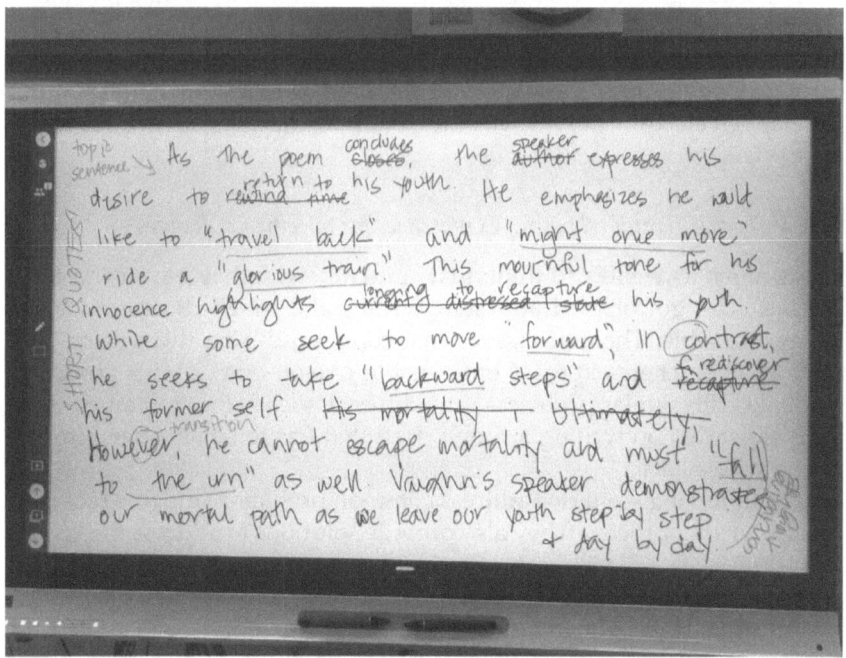

Figure 4.1. Collective paragraph on smart board Photo by Amy Matthusen

I feel like I understand more about what to do [for my essay] now. —Justin

I liked to see how you picked out a quote and used it. —Julisa

Quick Talk: Incremental Deadlines and the Flash Conference

Some students need shepherding through each step of the writing process. Higher-skilled, highly motivated students are off and running as soon as the assignment is in their hands. Most students, however, need either more guidance or more cheerleading to keep momentum, focus, and motivation. Especially for larger assignments, creating a series of incremental deadlines for smaller portions of the overall task keeps the class on track. Teachers differentiate deadlines depending on the needs of their students, their skill level, and the length of the class period. For many, the increment may be one to two paragraphs per class period for longer assignments to measure accountability.

Incremental timelines allow teachers to have "flash conferences" with students as they circulate the room. These conversations might only be a brief minute or two. Teachers can pull up a chair and ask the simplest of check-in questions: How's it going? Are you stuck at all? How can I help? Brief verbal check-ins can clarify points of confusion, allow for advice on further reading, or provide for a quick read and feedback on a portion of writing.

Alternatively, in an age when many teachers have students work through Google Docs, these quick check-ins and follow-up conversations can happen electronically when students share their documents for teachers to view.

Stay on Target: Troubleshooting Conferences for Specific Challenges

As much as we like to think that students, once they have completed outlines, can go forward and start writing the rough draft, this is not always possible. There are issues that come up during the writing process, as all teachers expect. Conferencing one-on-one or with groups of students with similar problems can address issues before too much energy is expended on writing a rough draft that has to be jettisoned in part or as a whole later.

The following scenarios address common problems students face during the writing process. They also provide solutions to address the issues.

Problem: The Detailed Outliner
Solution: Highlight and Index

Wendy loves to write detailed outlines, so much so that her outlines do not have much white space because they are so dense with words and sentences. Yet even with this detailed outline, Wendy always struggles to write a rough draft. She questions whether she selected the right topic. She wonders if she could find better evidence. Perhaps she did not understand what she read. Could the teacher look over her outline again?

For Wendy's teacher, this is an agonizing exercise. Wendy is hardworking, eager, and anxious to do well. Yet she is rather insecure at many stages of the writing process. Her questions are frequent and complicated so that answering every one of them means taking away time from other students during the drafting process. Her insecurities about her writing are misplaced. She is often on the right track and can produce engaging writing that showcases her critical thinking. The problem arises as Wendy has so many new ideas that she wants to put in the paper in addition to the information in the outline. The end result is more convoluted than coherent.

"Highlight and Index" is a task for Wendy to complete prior to meeting with her teacher. Wendy is instructed to highlight the main points of her essay and those that she thinks are the most interesting. On an index card, she answers the following questions:

- What is my thesis?
- Does my new idea/direction repeat a similar idea in the text?
- Does the new idea take away from my strongest points or strengthen them?
- Does the new idea mean that I have to write parts of my essay over?
- Does the new idea provide clarity or confusion?

Instead of going directly to her teacher, Wendy has to reflect on every new piece that she's trying to add to her already completed outline. For every new idea or direction, Wendy has to answer a few questions before she has a conversation with the instructor. It is an intentionally multistep process. What enables her to finally start writing her paper as opposed to being stuck conjuring new ideas and moving in new directions, without fully committing to any, is the result of this protocol, which she will eventually internalize.

Her teacher's hope is that this codified reflection will teach Wendy to analyze and discard before engaging in a conversation with the teacher. When Wendy is ready to speak with the teacher, she has more clarity and is able to identify more quickly what she should or should not add to the outline. Gone are the multiple new ideas that once poured out in a torrent.

WENDY: I did my index card.
MRS. CHERIAN: (laughs) This is a lot of writing on an index card.
WENDY: Yeah, I wanted to make sure I answered the questions.

MRS. CHERIAN: Looking at your outline, I see that you are proving that Antigone is selfish throughout the play. I like that you focused on her impact on the other characters.

WENDY: Yes, but I now think she is more noble than selfish. I want to add that Haemon thinks she is noble.

MRS. CHERIAN: That's true. You wrote on the index card that you think that Haemon's feelings take away from your overall argument. You also wrote it makes it more confusing because you have to add what Haemon says the public feels about Antigone.

WENDY: I don't think I want to write about Haemon. I think his love for her makes him biased. Do you think he's too biased?

MRS. CHERIAN: Do you think this addition to your outline would change the direction of your entire paper?

WENDY: Yes . . . but I think it is a good idea.

MRS. CHERIAN: Are you willing to change your thesis and paper for this idea?

WENDY: (long pause) Do you think I should? (long pause) No. I don't want to.

✍ Teacher Reflection

The Antigone *essay was the second major writing assignment of the sophomore year. By the spring semester, Wendy was able to have a conversation with herself and save herself from the agony of the "Highlight and Index" protocol. For Wendy, the super-detailed outline and the urge to keep adding to it was a form of anxious procrastination. For me, the protocol streamlines the conversations I have with Wendy without leading Wendy. —Mrs. Cherian*

Problem: The Skeleton Outliner
Solution: Transcribe This

There is always one. The student whose outline for a three-to-five-page paper does not even take up an entire loose-leaf page. There are no page numbers, and the points are so brief, they are mere fragments of ideas. For many years, Ms. Sullivan's advice was to say go and add more information to the outline. For Ms. Sullivan, this made sense because she likes to outline and plan. This is probably the case for a lot of teachers. While this solution seems feasible to an adult, for many students that skeleton outline is the culmination of every idea that they *think* they have about the assignment. For these students, more frequent conversations throughout the drafting process are required. And thanks to technology, the conversation can be transcribed and given to the student to use as an outline.

During Writing

The first students Ms. Sullivan speaks to during the rough-draft-writing process are the students who have minimal outlines. Often these are students who are less inclined to want to have a conversation with the instructor lest the teacher recognize their lack of ideas for the assignment. Many computers and laptops have transcription software; Ms. Sullivan likes to use the Voice Typing tool in Google Docs.

Before the conference, Ms. Sullivan turns on the Voice Typing tool to transcribe the conversation. The tool does not create a new line every time a different person is speaking, but it does allow the user to press enter to move to the next line and type in names (if desired) while the microphone stays on.

Danny is a student who hates to write but who loves to speak. He is so good at conversing that during conversations with his teacher over an assignment, he is able to draw out information from the teacher to help him complete the writing. He is always looking for *the* answer. The downside of this is that it is difficult to determine how much of his final product is his own critical thinking as opposed to ideas he has pulled out of his teacher. Students similar to Danny who are searching for the "right" answer benefit from conferences with specific questions to elicit responses from the student as opposed to answers and directions from the teacher. Knowing exactly what to ask Danny means that the teacher does not put too much of their own ideas into the conversation. It also puts the student on notice that the thinking has to be done by him.

This type of conference, where neither the student nor the teacher is taking notes, means that both parties are 100 percent engaged in the conversation. After the student and teacher engage in this conference, it is best to quickly look over the transcription and separate the different parts of the conversation by speaker. Print out or share the document with the student. It is ideal to print it out for the student so they can spend some time looking at what is written, highlighting information, and annotating on the transcription.

This process is empowering because students see that they are bringing ideas to the table. It is also a way to generate new ideas as opposed to trying to find the right answer. We want to encourage our students to think and be creative, to innovate, or to think critically and not just look at the instructor as an expert and parrot back those ideas in their writing. Before giving the printed document to the student, Mrs. Sullivan sends the student back to their desk to jot down from their own memory the ideas they shared in that conversation.

For the *Othello* writing assignment in tenth grade English, students must select a literary lens through which to examine the play. The "Transcribe This" conference is ideal for this assignment because Ms. Sullivan has to stay on script. The questions for the conversation are determined by the topic. Danny selected a feminist lens to analyze the play, and the questions are the common questions used for this type of analysis.

- What stereotypes of women are depicted in the text?
- Are they supportive or independent? Powerless or strong? Subservient or in control?
- If the female characters have any power, what kind is it? Political? Economic? Social? Psychological?
- How do the male characters talk about the female characters?
- How do the male characters treat the female characters?
- How do the female characters act toward the male characters?

MS. SULLIVAN: I'm interested in the lens you selected, Danny.
DANNY: Do you think it's the best one?
MS. SULLIVAN: Danny, you have to pick the lens you are most interested in. Let's go through these questions. What are some stereotypes in the play?
DANNY: I don't know.
MS. SULLIVAN: Your first body-paragraph bullet is about stereotypes. You just wrote the female character's names. Do you want to discuss each one?
DANNY: I don't know which stereotypes they are.
MS. SULLIVAN: Okay. Let's start with Desdemona. What are some ideas that you have about her?
DANNY: You said that she was educated but her father was angry at her.
MS. SULLIVAN: Forget what I said. Does she represent a stereotype in the play? What do you think? Maybe it would help to say what you notice about her and the other two women in the play.
DANNY: Desdemona seems nice, but Emilia seems angry all the time. Bianca only cares about men.
MS. SULLIVAN: Now tell me, for each one, how the character is represented that way.

✍ Teacher Reflection

These conversations don't need to happen right after outlining and right before they write the essay. The conversation does not even have to be about the entire writing assignment. I sometimes decide to have short conversations for every part of the essay right after certain students write the outline. Some students prefer to write their essays in parts. So it is beneficial to have a conversation about the introduction, then send the student out to work on the introduction. —Ms. Sullivan

WHAT ARE OTHER STUDENTS DOING?

Most students at this stage will be writing. If they wrap up the writing process early, students could do a self-reflection or edit based on the grading criteria, or proceed to another reading or writing task. At some point during the drafting phase, students can also participate in a peer review as a "critical friend," as described below.

Critical Friend Peer Edit

Incorporating peer-editing exercises into the writing process can help students provide feedback and consider potential revisions in their own writing. The concept of the "critical friend" is often used in educational journals and on teacher resource sites. Students can share a draft that is in its fledgling stages for a peer edit like this to get advice as they continue writing. The practice generally follows the construct below (and you could add time segments to these as needed):

1. While "critical friends" remain silent, the writer presents and describes his or her product. As they read, the "friends" may take notes related to the rubric, but they do not ask questions.
2. Presenters remain silent while the "friends" talk about the product as if the writer is not there. They might start with strengths, move on to improvements, and finally offer next steps. Teachers might create sentence starters to assist the conversation.
3. The writer can now respond to comments raised by the "critical friends" and discuss potential next steps with them.

These peer conferences help students improve a piece of writing. The practice can also build a community of writers in the classroom. Finally, it allows the teacher to pull struggling students into a conference while the other students complete their peer review.

SUMMARY

Drafting conferences are beneficial because they

- Emphasize the process over the product
- Keep students on track to meet deadlines
- Make visible the writing struggles of teachers and other students to build a strong classroom culture of writing

Students who benefit from conferences at this stage

- Struggle with longer writing tasks
- Want advice to "see if they're on the right track"
- Need a little extra encouragement to persevere

- Like to bounce ideas back and forth with someone

Effective conferences at this stage

- Offer (as always) specific suggestions for next steps
- Reference a schedule of incremental deadlines
- Demonstrate and acknowledge the "messiness" of writing

FIVE

Revision Conferences

Not that many years ago, Priya, a sweet ninth grader, told me, "Just tell me what I need to change." I was puzzled. Had I not told her? I looked down at her essay. Weren't my notes all over her paper? So I verbalized my notes to Priya. And in the very next essay assignment, Priya made the same mistakes again. I did not understand how a bright student could make repeated structural mistakes and errors in the presentation of her critical thinking. —Anita

English teachers provide written feedback on almost every essay and yet are perplexed when confronted with repeat offenders. Months may pass with a particular set of students with very little improvement. Teachers view longer writing assignments as an amalgamation of skills; students do not. For most students, each assignment exists in isolation, consisting of words organized into sentences and sentences organized into paragraphs that attempt to answer a particular prompt.

In actuality, writing is a set of skills that may be mastered, some incrementally and others exponentially, over the course of a school year. There is no fairy dust that makes some students better writers than others. Sure, there are more talented students, but every student can become a stronger writer over time once they view writing as skills to hone and the different levels of skill accomplishment as steps toward mastery.

Conferencing between the first draft and the final submission is prime conferencing time, as many teachers already know. What could be better? This is a sweet spot to acknowledge and appreciate a completed draft as well as an opportunity to polish and improve.

All students benefit from a conference between drafts; however, students who benefit most from conferences at this stage are those who rushed the first draft and did not read what they wrote before submitting the work. In addition, students who, like Priya, want to be told what to change, but who see each assignment as existing within a vacuum and thus do not improve their writing over the course of multiple assignments, benefit from draft conferences. Conferencing at this point is also beneficial to students who write well consistently, even on first drafts, and often receive feedback that consists of "Good job." Such students tend to see writing another draft as a waste of time. Conversations with these students can push them to think about style choices as opposed to structure and content.

EXAMPLES AND PRACTICES FOR REVISION CONFERENCES

This chapter provides tools, strategies, and examples to assist with conferencing between drafts for students who are at different levels of mastery. The following examples foster repeated reflection on both the student's and the teacher's part during the revision process. The conferences are not just student–teacher conversations; rather, they are exercises in collegial conversations among students. Peer-editing rounds and writing groups are effective when students trust the expertise of others and when they know the conversations will be more encouraging than critical. Lastly, the inclusion of rubrics at this stage integrates specificity and objectivity.

Let's Talk: Student Identification of Conversation Focus

A "Let's Talk" conference is a simple conversation driven by the student's needs and concerns. The teacher may or may not have read the student's draft. Reading is not necessary per se. The student completes a simple questionnaire similar to the one below prior to meeting with the teacher.

- The prompt is about . . .
- My one-sentence answer to the prompt is . . .
- I struggled with . . .
- I have a question about . . .

Once the student reflects on the writing, he or she knows what to focus on in the conversation. The instructor does not drive the conversation and sits back in order to provide space. The questionnaire is turned in so the student can express the most pressing concern at that moment. It's natural for teachers to control the direction of the conversation without meaning to. That unconscious driving of the conversation means the teacher identifies the problems and provides the solution. The student is left to wonder if they are unable to determine what they need to focus on, and they become less trusting of their own instincts about their writing.

In this conference, the student directs attention to sections of the writing that have become problematic. Together, both parties problem solve the issue once the student has expressed everything he or she wrote. It is a brief workshop that could be used in conjunction with later or earlier peer review. Consider the "Let's Talk" model a low-stress, easy talk. This model may also be used in conversations between students.

Tell Me: Providing Silence for Expression

The "Tell Me" protocol is a variation on the "Let's Talk." This is another exercise in listening. The teacher is silent and takes notes. Do not ask any questions except the initial "What do you want to tell me about this assignment?" It is human nature to speak into the silence, but the teacher has to take a step back and not lead the student. The silence is to encourage the student to share whatever they want.

Mrs. Johnson takes notes as the student shares. Afterward, she says thank you and repeats all the points mentioned by the student and asks, "Of these, what do you want to address now?"

Mrs. Johnson shares that this protocol takes every conversation she has with a student in a different direction. Often, Mrs. Johnson comes into the conference with issues she wants to address. Yet every conversation takes a different turn. The student feels they have received personalized attention driven by their concerns, while Mrs. Johnson gathers data not influenced by her own perception of the student's need. While our understanding of a student's strengths and weaknesses is valuable, it is not a complete picture because we are missing the student's evaluation of the work.

In "Tell Me" conferences, students express confusion about what needs to be revised, struggle to evaluate their work beyond conventions, and even confess that they have not actually reread their work.

Revision Stations: Small-Group Conferencing

A formidable obstacle in attempting conferences in middle or high school classrooms is trying to have individual conversations with every student. This lesson structure allows for small-group conferences, permitting some degree of individualized conversation and instruction. In a classroom where there are tables or desks arranged together, these can be constructed as stations with focused work at each table for a prescribed amount of time.

In Mr. Tendilla's classroom, he works with a co-teacher and has thirty freshmen of varying skill levels. After reading students' rough drafts, he considers targeted mini-lessons or exercises to address deficits or reinforce important skills that will help guide essay revisions. Mr. Tendilla's classes are forty minutes long with a set of six tables and five students at each table. Along with his co-teacher, Mrs. Arteaga, he divides the class into six groups. Each student will need a hard copy of his or her rough draft for this lesson.

Students spend approximately twelve minutes at each station, ensuring that they see at least one teacher for small-group conferencing. For example, students move from station 1 to station 2 to station 3 (and

Figure 5.1. Forty-Minute-Class Station Activity

Station 1A: Group 1
Highlighter Check: Students review their papers to make sure they have all the necessary components using a set of different colored highlighters. This could look something like this:
Blue: Thesis and topic sentences
Pink: Quotes
Yellow: Analysis of quotes
Green: Transition words
What students highlight can vary, but noticing these components of the paper will demonstrate points that may need revision. A model paper on the table could be used as a guide.

Station 1B: Group 4
This second group of students also works on the highlighter check.

Station 2A: Group 2
Quote Intro Practice (or a similar targeted skill): Students review samples of various word choices and phrasings that could be used to introduce a quote. With these models, they return to their papers and double-check their own quote introductions.

Station 2B: Group 5
This second group of students also reviews quote introductions.

Station 3A: Group 3
Small-Group Conferencing: Students in this group read and annotate two different sample paragraphs of submitted essays (with names removed), paying particular attention to quote analysis, a difficult skill. Mr. Tendilla then guides discussion on the samples: What did you notice? What made one sample stronger or weaker than the other? What questions does this raise for your own paper?
This small-group conferencing is useful for helping students see the qualities of stronger analysis through authentic conversations about actual writing from their classmates.

Station 3B: Group 6
Small-Group Conferencing: This second group of students engages in small-group conferencing with Mr. Tendilla's co-teacher, Mrs. Arteaga. They follow the same pattern as described for Group 3.

station 3 students move to station 1). This lesson organization has the benefit of seeing students in a small group of approximately five students. In this setting, shyer students are more likely to speak up and ask questions. The best part of this option for conferencing is that every student is captured at least briefly for a conversation before undertaking a revision.

Another teacher, Ms. Ahmed, uses a similar lesson for her section of thirty juniors. Ms. Ahmed's classes are a bit longer, with a full sixty-minute period, but she does not have a co-teacher. The stations in her class follow the structure below; the first three are similar to Mr. Tendilla's, but with more time, each group spends approximately ten minutes at six different stations on six specific tasks, eventually cycling through to see Ms. Ahmed for small-group discussion and conferencing.

Figure 5.2. Sixty-Minute-Class Station Activity

Station 1:
Highlighter Check: Students review their papers to make sure they have all the necessary components using a set of different colored highlighters. This could look something like this:
Blue: Thesis and topic sentences
Pink: Quotes
Yellow: Analysis of quotes
Green: Transition words
What students highlight can vary, but noticing these components of the paper will demonstrate points that may need revision. A model paper on the table could be used as a guide.

Station 2:
Quote Intro Practice (or a similar targeted skill): Students review samples of various word choices and phrasings that could be used to introduce a quote. With these models, they return to their papers and double-check their own quote introductions.

Station 3:
Small-Group Conferencing: Students in this group read and annotate two different sample paragraphs of submitted essays (with names removed), paying particular attention to quote analysis, a difficult skill. Ms. Ahmed then guides discussion on the samples: What did you notice? What made one sample stronger or weaker

Station 4:
Self-Edit with Rubric: Students review their papers with a checklist rubric and give themselves a grade. They then write a bulleted to-do list as a revision plan guided by the rubric.

Station 5:
Peer-Edit Thesis Statement. The thesis statement is the most important sentence of an essay. With a partner at the station, students read each other's thesis statements for clarity, specificity, and any other criteria relevant to the task.

Station 6:
Reflective Writing: Students engage in a quick-write reflecting on the challenges of the assignment. They may also suggest additional resources they would like for future similar assignments or offer suggestions for adjusting instruction for future related lessons.

than the other? What questions does this raise for your own paper?
This small-group conferencing is useful for helping students see the qualities of stronger analysis through authentic conversations about actual writing from their classmates.

Technology-Driven Alternative: Audio Comments

An alternative with many of the benefits of conferencing is audio comments on papers. Turnitin.com, Kaizena, VoiceThread, and other tools allow teachers to make audio recordings. Mrs. Mercedes finds it difficult to conference with all the students in her senior English class, so she alternates conferencing and audio comments among students.

When she reads a student's draft, she pauses after each paragraph and adds a little more to the recording, moving through the paper paragraph by paragraph. She pretends the student is sitting next to her as she records, as if in a conference. When students listen to the comments, she asks them to take out a pen and paper to take notes as they listen.

Ms. Mercedes's students have given her positive feedback about the audio recordings. Many of them feel the audio comments are more understandable and engaging than written feedback. Although abstractly students know teachers sit down with their papers to grade them, the audio comments bring home the reality of the time spent with the paper and the thought that goes into providing feedback. Her students often produce better revisions after hearing audio feedback as compared to revisions based on written feedback. While a one-on-one conference is still a more desirable practice, this option affords many of the same benefits without the demands of class-time logistics.

TRANSCRIPT OF AUDIO COMMENTS

Hi, Tenzin! It's Ms. Mercedes. I'm going to read through your paper and say something about each paragraph, so please take out a piece of paper and a pen and take notes as you listen. Then let me know in class if anything I'm saying is unclear.

So I just read through your introduction. It's on the right track, but it's a little short. Please add a couple sentences of an overview of your paper to fill out the paragraph more.

I also read through your first body paragraph. I think you've done a nice job of selecting quotes here. Your first quote, in particular, works well for your argument [reads the quote]. You have nice analysis after the quote as well because it looks at the specific language in the quote and explains why the rhetorical choices are purposeful. The second quote, however, is not given the same attention [reads quote]. This quote needs more specific analysis to work well for your argument. For example, some of the word choices in this quote [reads words] would be great to discuss in more detail. Let me take a look at your next body paragraph on appeals to pathos.

Just read through your second paragraph. These quotes work well for your paper, but it's just a little light. What I'm noticing is this first quote you chose is a bit short. Perhaps if you add an additional sentence from the text before or after this line—then you'll have a little more to analyze and more to talk about. Let me take a look at your next body paragraph on appeal to logos.

Okay, just finished reading. I really have similar comments here as well. You've done a nice job of selecting quotes. . . . It's the analysis afterward that needs some attention and development. I also see that you're not quite at the two-page length requirement, so you'll need to add to paragraphs to get there. I think after you add another line of analysis to the parts we focused on, you'll be there.

If I can clarify anything I've said or offer you advice as you revise, please let me know & I'll see you in class.

A Skills Conference: Focusing on Substance with Common Language

A skills conference between the rough and final version of writing demands that the students know the skills assessed. Rubrics create a common language. While rubrics seem like an obvious amalgamation of skills and task expectations, these are not necessarily understood by students. You might provide feedback by using rubrics and then wonder why the new version of a writing piece is so similar to the earlier version. This is often because students do not understand the language of the rubric. As a class, work to break down, alter, and streamline the rubric.

Have groups identify the skills assessed by a particular category of a rubric. Then have them change the language so it is simple and not restricted by pedagogical jargon. Afterward, each of the groups can present to the class a revised version of their section. Or have separate periods focus on a particular category; each whole class can then agree on the revised version. The teacher will then create a more student-friendly and more easily understood rubric.

From this, you can create a more precise breakdown of the skills in a style that is not a grid. Present the skills and the various degrees of mastery as levels. In figure 5.3, the highest level is a four. Once the teacher checks off the level the student is currently at, the student will be able to see what the next steps are.

All this is a segue into the idea that a conference about a specific skill deficiency is only insightful for a student when they understand the skills to be mastered for a writing task. A specific skills rubric focuses the conversation. Most often, five minutes is all teachers can devote to a student, so complete the grading and the rubric before the conference. When the student arrives at the meeting, the instructor hands their rough draft to them and asks them to skim over their writing to refresh their memory while the teacher looks over the completed rubric. Then commence with a brief conversation. Focus on the categories of skills that are high leverage for the student.

Questions to ask:

- Based on the rubric, what skills do you see that you progressed with?
- I see that this (insert skill) was problematic for you. What is your understanding of what you were supposed to do?
- How can we move to the next mastery level?

The teacher shares what the student did well and has the student acknowledge their strengths. A strength is anything the student does better relative to other skills on the rubric; even if that number is a two out of four. Young writers need to see positives before they can be receptive to more critical commentary.

Next, select the highest-leverage skill to discuss. Analysis? Organization? A clear thesis to direct the writing? A skills rubric is detailed and, initially, is unwieldy to grade with, but the upside is that there is less red pen bleeding on the student document.

A skills rubric can grow as the school year progresses and the assignments become more complicated. Conversely, as certain skills become more ingrained and more students master the skills, those skills may be dropped from the rubric.

A skills rubric should prompt the student writer to ask, How do I get *there* from *here*? The conference should clear up confusion and provide clarity while allowing space for conversation.

While the example in figure 5.3 includes a tally of points and a rough draft grade, note that there is not a need for a grade percentage based on the points. A rough draft could just be a completion grade in a category. A draft is just that—a draft. Some students are more receptive to feedback when there is not a perceived punitive grade attached.

Rough Draft Rubric

Name_____   Assignment: Rough Draft

Points Earned ____/ 52   Overall Grade_____
Essay Structure Overall

Introduction Paragraph Organization ☐ 4: Well- written, interesting introduction that is a complete inverted triangle format. ☐ 3: Contains all the parts of the inverted (upside down) triangle for the introduction with a clear thesis (Hook, Bridge, Context, Thesis). ☐ 2: Relates to the essay topic/ prompt but does not contain all the parts.   1: Introduction lacks focus and reader unclear about what will be proven in essay. ☐ 0: Needs to write an introduction.
Development of an Argument in a Thesis Statement ☐ 4: Clearly indicates what will be proven in essay and provides list of points. ☐ 3: Includes a thesis statement but points are not specified. ☐ 2: Writes a thesis statement that responds to the prompt but not in correct location. ☐ 1: Thesis statement is missing or not related to rest of essay.
Conclusion ☐ 4: Answers the "So What?" and adds insights about human nature or society. Re-words the thesis & summarizes key points. ☐ 3: Re-words the thesis, summarizes key points made in the essay and includes the "So What" ☐ 2: Restates same thesis from introduction thesis in the conclusion. ☐ 1: Needs to write a conclusion.   ____/12 points

Body Paragraph Structure

Topic Sentence ☐ 4: Topic sentence is a sophisticated statement of what will be argued in the paragraph. ☐ 3: Topic sentence indicates what will be argued in the paragraph. ☐ 2: Topic sentence repeats same idea as thesis in the introduction. ☐ 1: Missing a topic sentence or topic sentence includes evidence.
Supporting Sentences in a Paragraph

Figure 5.3   Rough draft rubric

If there are concerns about how to direct a conversation in a conference with a student who needs a conference when others might not, use the assessment's rubric to guide the discussion. The option in figure 5.4 is a classic grid rubric but breaks down the usual dense text into bulleted skills within each category. The last row was set aside for the skill taught for the assignment. The provided example is for an extended paragraph response.

- ❏ 4: All sentences support the topic sentence.
- ❏ 3: Some sentences support the topic sentence.
- ❏ 2: Most sentences seem disconnected to topic sentence.
- ❏ 1: Sentences and ideas do not prove idea in topic sentence. Consider changing topic sentence.

_____/8 points

Evidence & Analysis

Integration of Evidence into Writing
- ❏ 4: Quote flows naturally and is integrated into the grammar and structure of student's sentence. The context is provided for the quote (Who said what to whom and when)
- ❏ 3: Embeds quote with a sentence starter to introduce the quote.
- ❏ 2: Writes quote directly from the text. Quote is not introduced.
- ❏ 1: Needs to quote from the text. Find evidence, please.

Interpretation of Evidence (Analysis)
- ❏ 4: Well-thought out or interesting examination of evidence. Analysis goes well beyond a literal level.
- ❏ 3: Analyzes/ breaks down evidence. Some analysis is literal.
- ❏ 2: Briefly analyzes the evidence. Some parts are only partially explained. Superficial explanation; dig deeper
- ❏ 1: Only summarizes evidence.

Connecting the evidence to the topic sentence in the body paragraph (Analysis)
- ❏ 4: Clearly proves the point mentioned in the topic sentence with multiple pieces of evidence. Connections are interesting.
- ❏ 3: Explains the connection between the topic sentence and chosen evidence.
- ❏ 2: Identifies briefly the connection between topic sentence and chosen evidence. Quotes might be too long.
- ❏ 1: Needs to explain the connection of the evidence to the idea in the topic sentence.

Concluding Link Sentences (Analysis)
- ❏ 4: Makes connections between the ideas in the paragraph to the overall essay thesis and hints at ideas in the next paragraph.
- ❏ 3: Connects ideas in the paragraph to the thesis.
- ❏ 2: Repeats topic sentence of the body paragraph.
- ❏ 1: Unclear or missing link.

Sourcing of Evidence
- ❏ 4: Uses assigned, academic format to cite the quotes with a period after the citation(use line #s for _Antigone_) Ex: (lines 334-345). All citations are after the quote.
- ❏ 3: Identifies source information but format is incorrect.
- ❏ 2: Identifies source information, but the location of citation is not correct.
- ❏ 1: Needs to identify source of information.

_____/25 points

Style & Conventions

Use of transition words
- ❏ 3: Varies use of transition words establishing logical connections between sentences and paragraphs.
- ❏ 2: Uses some transition words.
- ❏ 1: Needs to use transition words to prevent sudden, jarring mental leaps between sentences and paragraphs.
  * See ELA Reference book for examples of transition words.

Grammar/ Punctuation/Spelling
- ❏ 4: 0-3 mistakes. Thank you for proofreading your work.
- ❏ 3: 2- 5 mistakes. Mistakes do not hinder understanding.
- ❏ 2: 5-10 mistakes.
- ❏ 1: Many mistakes. Some sentences are confusing.

_____/7 points

Figure 5.3   Rough draft rubric (continued)

Figure 5.4 "Se Habla Espanol" and *Born a Crime*: Focus Skill Quote Integration Rubric and Analysis

	Excellent 100–90	Good 89–75	Proficient 74–65	Needs Improvement 64–0
Main Idea/ Topic Sentence	• Answers the prompt question completely.	• Mostly answers the prompt question	• Somewhat answers the prompt question. • Answer might be only partially related.	• Does not answer the prompt question. • Answer is unrelated or confusing. • Main idea/topic sentence missing. • Paragraph starts with evidence.
Evidence	• You have multiple pieces of evidence (quotes) used in your paragraph to strongly support the argument. • They are well introduced and properly cited. • Evidence supports and connects to the main idea/topic sentence well.	• You have multiple pieces of evidence (quotes) used in your paragraph to support the argument. • They are introduced and cited.	• You have evidence (quotes) used in your paragraph to support your argument. • Evidence is related to prompt. • Evidence not as well introduced or cited.	• The evidence is not related. • There are better examples of evidence to support the main idea/topic sentence. • Missing citation. • Incorrect citation format.

	Excellent 100–90	Good 89–75	Proficient 74–65	Needs Improvement 64–0
Focus Skill: Analysis	• You have analysis following each piece of evidence introduced. • Engaging ideas. • Insightful connections made between *BAC* and "Se Habla." • Completely answers writer's purpose and what is said about society.	• You have an analysis following each piece of evidence introduced. • Analysis shows critical thinking. • Answers all questions. • Somewhat answer all questions about writer's purpose and what is said about society.	• Analysis is present but brief. • There is analysis for each evidence with some critical thinking. • Answers one: writer's purpose **OR** what is said about society.	• Analysis is missing or unrelated to the evidence you presented. • Only paraphrases evidence. • Has many unanswered questions. • Does not address deeper analysis questions (neither writer's purpose **NOR** what is said about society).
Link	• Link explains **fully** how the evidence and analysis prove the answer in the main idea/topic sentence.	• Link **connects** the evidence and analysis to prove the answer in the main idea/topic sentence.	• Your link attempts to connect your analysis and evidence to prove the answer in the main idea/topic sentence but **some ideas/information are left out**.	• Link **does not make an accurate connection** to the main idea/topic sentence. • Your link is missing or confusing. • Link is just a repeat of the main idea/topic sentence.
Focus Skill: Quote Integration	• Uses a signal phrase that is sophisticated. • Uses specific words/phrases as evidence instead of longer quotes. • Selects evidence that reinforces ideas in analysis and the main idea/topic sentence. • Provides informative context for the evidence.	• Uses a signal phrase that is **NOT** "stated" or "said." • Uses [ ] or … (ellipse). • Provides context. • Quote reinforces ideas in rest of paragraph.	• Uses a signal word. • Has a basic quote introduction. • Has some context. • Needs to find stronger evidence.	• Does not include any context. • Only paraphrases evidence. • Quote is too long. • **Does not** have any of the focus skills elements: brackets [ ] ellipses … smaller quote

Excellent 100–90	Good 89–75	Proficient 74–65	Needs Improvement 64–0
• Evidence flows in a sophisticated manner with student's own words.			

WHAT ARE OTHER STUDENTS DOING?

Conferences during the revision process might be longer. As such, what the other students are doing should be more involved. This could be the best time to engage the students in peer-editing strategies.

Writing Groups: Using Peers as a Source of Authentic Feedback

Calling a group of students a writer's group changes the energy. In a classroom culture of conferencing, peer comments are vital in the revision process—though truth be told, unwelcome initially. Every student wants feedback from the "expert"—the adult in the room. While sometimes it is feasible to be the expert for five classes of thirty-two students, other times it is an impossible task.

Writer's groups resolve some of the issue by generating a sense of intimacy in a small group of three as they workshop writing pieces. A caveat: writer's groups are not for the beginning of the school year. Take the time to intuit the developing dynamics and relationships in a class. Then, describe to the class the fostering and trusting nature of a writing group. Finally, explain to students that while it is not possible to accommodate every request, you do want to know whom they would choose to be in their group of three.

The groups may be aligned based on partner requests or skill levels (either heterogenous or homogenous), but it is vital that a group wants to work together. Maiko and Kaley can never work together due to an altercation in their freshman year. In their sophomore year, Mrs. Johnson never places the girls in the same group. That lesson was learned the difficult way the second month of school when Maiko spent an entire period with her head down to avoid eye contact and conversation with Kaley. Mrs. Johnson only learned of the bad blood between the two girls because of a chance conversation with the girls' advisory (homeroom) teacher.

Writing groups should not be formed in the first month of school, so give yourself time to learn the possible history of students from observations or direct questions to past teachers. Each class has its own dynamics and unspoken rules of engagement. Take time to observe and note what seems to be working through small-stakes pair and group tasks.

All writing groups must decide on a code of behavior regarding responsibility, preparation, and language used in critiques. The writer's group may work together at any stage of writing. It is helpful at the revision stage because two sets of eyes review one person's writing at a time.

The teacher may present a mini-lesson on a specific skill. The writer's group takes turns looking at each other's papers through that lens. The teacher can also visit each of the groups. In a full class, perhaps there are ten groups. It is feasible to see almost all if not all the groups in meetings of three to five minutes.

A well-functioning writer's group decreases the feeling of isolation while increasing motivation and confidence. Furthermore, a writer's group means that students can experience small successes when they take turns being an expert on an aspect of writing or revision.

Peer-to-Peer in Rounds: Encouraging Written Student Conversation

Most students struggle with other students looking over their work. Part of the concern is feeling embarrassed; however, most of the feeling is rooted in the idea that peers have little to offer in the way of actionable feedback. Add to that the fear that the wrong peer will evaluate the work. Stronger writers might not value feedback from a perceived lower-skilled writer.

Peer-to-peer conversations are beneficial, but not as much when the same student reviews an entire paper. Peer review in rounds demands that every section (every paragraph even) is read by a different student. For the tenth grade research paper, students fill out a peer evaluation sheet that indicates the topic and the thesis. The evaluation sheet (see figure 5.5) and the research paper travel every paragraph in a group of five or six students. The student who evaluates the introduction is not the same student who evaluates body paragraph two or three. The research paper is viewed by multiple students and thus addresses some of the belief that peer review is a waste of time for higher-level students while providing multiple samples of stronger writing for weaker English students to view.

For nonessay writing, students will read the entire piece and look for story or poetic elements.

If the instructor chooses, the peer evaluation sheets may be collected, reviewed, and used to identify students who need further assistance. The sheets provide vital information without the necessity of looking over every student's work if time between drafts is brief. Specifically helpful is the ability to discern which students could be conferenced with as a group in an effort to save additional time.

Do not feel the pressure to collect these sheets. Problems that peers usually identify are simple enough that the student writer can resolve the issues independently. In addition, the next version of the paper that the teacher encounters will have most of the structural and convention issues addressed. This means that student–teacher conversations will be less caught up in minutiae.

English 10 (2019)   Research Paper Writer_____

Peer Edit Sheet for Research Paper

WRITE YOUR THESIS HERE:

Write yes or no for the sections included	What was done well?	What needs to be improved? What was confusing? Do you have suggestions on how to improve?
Introduction (Paragraph #1) ____Hook sentence - Grab the reader's attention ____Transition to topic -Identified the topic & clarified terms and scope/context of your paper ____Provide some background information on the topic (short) ____Thesis Statement - (Topic + opinion/ call to action + three reasons why) ____Are there spelling or grammar mistakes?		
Background (Paragraph #2) Provide background information on the topic/ issue. **Write YES or NO below** ____Does the writer explain the topic well? ____Does the writer explain the who/what/when/where? ____Are you confused? ____Do you feel informed enough?		What questions do you have about the topic you wish the writer had answered?

____Did they establish there is a problem or issue ____Are there spelling or grammar mistakes?		
Check off the parts that the writer included	What was done well?	What needs to be improved? What was confusing? Do you have suggestions on how to improve?
Claim/ Reason #1 **Write YES or NO below** Did the writer include... ____**Claim** #1 as topic sentence (a specific claim) ____**Evidence**/ Data/ Fact to support the claim? ____**Analysis** (Explain how the evidence/data/ quote connects to your reason/claim? ____**Counterclaim** (What does the other side think about the specific claim you are making?) ____**Rebuttal** (Did they specifically respond to the counterclaim?) ____Did the writer stay on topic? ____Are there any spelling or grammar mistakes?		
Claim/ Reason #2 **Write YES or NO below** Did the writer include... ____**Claim** #1 as topic sentence (a specific claim) ____**Evidence**/ Data/ Fact to support the claim? ____**Analysis** (Explain how the evidence/data/ quote connects to your reason/claim)? ____**Counterclaim** (What does the other side think about the specific claim you are making?)		

Figure 5.5   Research paper peer-edit sheet

____ **Rebuttal** (Did they specifically respond to the counterclaim?) ____ Did the writer stay on topic? ____ Are there any spelling or grammar mistakes?		
Check off the parts that the writer included	What was done well?	What needs to be improved? What was confusing? Do you have suggestions on how to improve?
Claim/ Reason #3 **Write YES or NO below** Did the writer include... ____ **Claim** #1 as topic sentence (a specific claim) ____ **Evidence**/ Data/ Fact to support the claim? ____ **Analysis** (Explain how the evidence/data/ quote connects to your reason/claim)? ____ **Counterclaim** (What does the other side think about the specific claim you are making?) ____ **Rebuttal** (Did they specifically respond to the counterclaim?) ____ Did the writer stay on topic? ____ Are there any spelling or grammar mistakes?		
Check off the parts that the writer included	What was done well?	What needs to be improved? What was confusing? Do you have suggestions on how to improve?
Conclusion ____ Is there a restatement of thesis? ____ Is there a review of claims?		
____ Did the writer provide solutions or next steps? OR ____ Is there a statement of what would happen if the reader does not take your position? ____ Is the conclusion interesting? ____ Are there any spelling or grammar mistakes?		

Figure 5.5   Research paper peer-edit sheet (continued)

Love Letters: Writing Friendly Feedback

This practice is inspired by Kate Hope at Arizona State University. "Love Letters" work well in writing groups. Instructors want to write extensive feedback, yet after marking for organization, grammar, punctuation, and analysis, that simple paragraph at the end seems so daunting. Also, after spending time trying to find what is wrong (not our constant intent, but it happens), it is difficult to muster the correct tone and words to be constructive and nurturing.

Instruct students to bring two copies of their writing to the group. Each student silently reads and responds to the other two students' writing. The love letter should follow a specific format. There are multiple ways for the the students to write the letter, but whatever the format is, instruct students to stay within those guidelines.

A possible format:

> Dear ...
> The central point I think you are trying to make is ...
> What I enjoyed reading was ...

> An interesting point you made was . . .
> Some questions I have are . . .
> The strongest part of the writing was . . .
> Thank you for allowing me to read the . . .

The members of the writing group do not mark up the writing. They are not looking for spelling, grammar, or organizational mistakes. The love letter is part of creating a dynamic that will hopefully morph into a more critical but still nurturing relationship.

An assignment does not need to be completed to give letter-form feedback. The students below provided and received feedback on the introduction and background/problem-establishment paragraphs.

Giving feedback in a letter format allowed me to be more extensive in how I think they can edit their paper. For example, rather than just stating the student has a hook, I could tell the student what I liked or didn't like about the hook. I think this is what also made getting feedback in letter form good for me. My peer was able to pinpoint exact spots in my essay which needed editing rather than just telling what I had or didn't. —Taliyah

I enjoyed giving feedback this way because I felt like I was helping them know what they are doing right and what they need to improve on. When I got my feedback letter back it felt like they were helping me and encouraging me to improve rather than only judging my work. It also showed me that my topic was interesting and worth writing. —Fiama

I like doing this as a letter format feels more heartfelt. One is more truthful when writing in this form. You know that the other person is trying to help you succeed as you give feedback for the other person. —Harrison

SUMMARY

Revision conferences are beneficial because they

- Provide specific, actionable feedback
- Enable students to view multiple samples of writing in peer-to-peer review rounds
- Force students to drive the conversation once they reflect on the completed draft
- Allow students to review their writing as a whole product

Students who benefit from conferences at these stages are students who

- Want specific commentary
- Started but are unable to finish the first draft

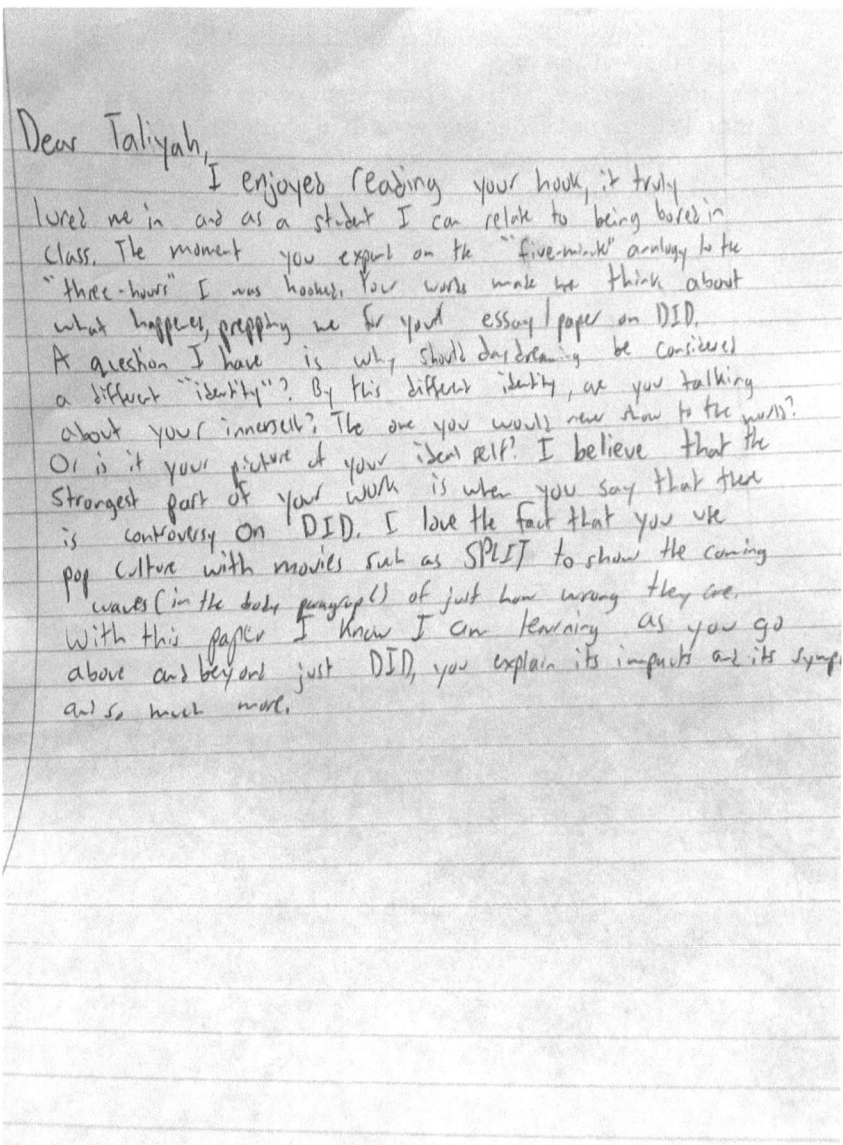

Figure 5.6 Love letter sample

- Need to verbalize concerns
- Want to workshop their writing
- Need help seeing the strengths in their writing

Effective conferences at this stage

- Put the onus of preparation and direction of the conference on the student, asking them to review and explain how they will use feedback for the revision
- Offer specific strategies based on student needs and requests
- Continue to acknowledge that growth in writing is part of a process
- Have a common language through the use of rubrics for skills-focused conferences

SIX
Reflective and Portfolio Conferences

Conferences have helped me get used to acknowledging what I need to do to improve my grade rather than grading decisions only made by the teacher.
—Alexandria, high school senior

Conferencing on major writing tasks provides substantial benefits for improving student writing on individual assignments. Ideally, these conversations around areas for improvement transfer to other writing contexts. Encouraging this transfer is further fostered by reflective conferences that look at a range of assignments over time.

A summative conference affords its own set of benefits. Students are offered a sense of accomplishment by acknowledging a volume of work from a whole unit, term, or year. Ideally, this may also enhance their view of themselves as writers and scholars. Marking-period or portfolio conferences allow us to climb out of the minutiae of the line edits on a single assignment to broader conversations about general practices and strategies applicable beyond one class's assignments and goals.

Finally, these conferences are opportunities for students to reflect on growth and advocate for themselves. Students often leave our classrooms with very little real-world experience in speaking about their strengths and weaknesses in a formal setting. These skills and practices could be invaluable in interviews for colleges, employers, or other opportunities. Independent of specific outcomes in English classrooms, this exposure and practice can be the first step to students gaining confidence for these future conversations when the stakes are higher.

EXAMPLES AND PRACTICES FOR REFLECTIVE CONFERENCES

A reflective conference permits a wider view for both teacher and student to celebrate ongoing successes and strategize for persistent challenges. This chapter offers examples and strategies for this type of conference. To begin, we consider a reflective conversation on a single assignment. From there, the lens widens to consider portfolio conferences that examine a body of student work. Finally, there is a consideration of marking-period conferences, which offer students the opportunity to review a term's worth of work and recommend a grade based on established criteria.

Questions for portfolio and reflective conferences:

- What strengths do you notice? What are you proud of? What would you like to highlight that demonstrates something you've learned?
- What were some challenges? What do you wish you had done differently? How can I help you or other students who struggle with a similar challenge?
- For single-assignment conferences: What do you want to remember about this assignment (strengths or weaknesses) for future assignments?
- For portfolio conferences: What are the consistent aspects of your writing? What trends do you notice about the feedback you've received?
- For marking-period conferences: Based on your work and the qualities highlighted on the grade agreement (standards scores, attention to feedback, progress, and completion of work), what grade do you feel you deserve?

Postgame Analysis: Reviewing the First Major Writing Assignment

As teachers, we often assume students understand and appreciate the overarching purpose of assignments. Stepping back for a moment to evaluate whether or not an assignment achieved its purpose is valuable for both a student writer and a teacher honing instruction. These conversations manifest misunderstandings, give the teacher ideas for supplemental resources or lessons, and help students clarify next steps. A perfect opportunity for this is after the first major writing assessment.

The conversation below from Ms. Jamal's tenth grade English class is based on a thematic essay assignment analyzing betrayal in Toni Morrison's *Sula*. Ms. Jamal and Jun Hao review the writing process as a whole with consideration for the skills and resources that could be used with future projects. We rarely take the time to step back and evaluate the process as a whole. Finally, these conversations hone students' metacognitive skills and their view of themselves as writers.

MS. JAMAL: What do you think went well with this assignment?

JUN HAO: I think I picked out good examples. Especially the example of Sula sleeping with Jude and Eva killing Plum.

MS. JAMAL: Why do you feel those worked well?

JUN HAO: They are clear betrayals. It's just wrong. Sula sleeps with her best friend's husband—that is too much. You cannot do that to a best friend.

MS. JAMAL: What was difficult about this assignment?

JUN HAO: Sometimes I don't know how to connect them. The examples. The analysis is hard, and what else to say about the examples.

MS. JAMAL: I can understand that. That's really the most difficult skill for any writer trying this. What do you think I could do to help you more with that? Any resources or advice you might like?

JUN HAO: Maybe some examples could help. Sometimes I just don't know what else to say.

MS. JAMAL: That's a good idea. I'll get some samples before we write an assignment; some sentence starters for how to begin analysis sentences might help too. Please keep asking me in class if you're stuck.

Teacher Reflection

Jun Hao is struggling with a common challenge for any writer here: the analysis. However, the challenge of this skill and related strategies may not be explicit to him without stepping back from the work and discussing it in a conference. This conference also provides me with some ideas to incorporate before the next major writing assignment. Models, sentence starters, and other examples can help Jun Hao and other students to get ideas for expanding and developing analysis in paragraphs. —Ms. Jamal

The Collected Works: Portfolio Conferences

In a tenth grade English class focused on rhetoric, Mr. Miller has asked students to prepare for portfolio conferences; in particular, he has asked students to review the rhetorical analysis essays they've written so far. The benefit of conferencing with portfolios is the expansive view it allows for a range of writing over a longer period of time. From this view, it is easier to see trends of strengths, challenges, and progress. The conversation below is with a "medium-level" student reflecting on a few essays collectively. Questions in the conference replicate the written responses students prepared in advance.

MR. MILLER: What's working with the rhetorical analysis essays? What are you feeling a little more confident about now?

SUE: I feel like I've improved with my thesis statements. [Sue uses a couple examples from her portfolio to demonstrate.] I can say the author's purpose better and explain it more.

MR. MILLER: When you look back on your essays, do you notice any consistent challenges?

SUE: It's really hard to explain and connect language to purpose. When I look at my essays, I feel like I'm always summarizing.

MR. MILLER: That's the hardest part of rhetorical analysis: making sure you are providing analysis, not summary. [At this point, they review some examples of quote analysis in different essays from the portfolio.] Try following a quote with "in order to" followed by an action verb like "persuade," "condemn," or "draw attention to." For example, the author makes this comparison in order to persuade her audience that . . . etc.

Sue and Mr. Miller close the conference by highlighting the progress made since the beginning of the year based on essays in the portfolio.

✍ Teacher Reflection

Some students will need additional scaffolds and trackers to organize their works for a portfolio. I'm thinking of setting up hanging files in a crate where students keep work. Electronic portfolios is another. I'm also considering an idea that shyer students may like, a video or mock conference to see how they should prepare. We may also have portfolio conferences that can be held before a panel of teachers or peers for higher stakes and greater accountability. —Mr. Miller

Although it is difficult to replicate with only a written transcript, the conversation between Sue and Mr. Miller has significance as a venue to recognize progress in writing over time. Mr. Miller and Sue can look at the nascent attempts at a difficult writing task and contrast them with the stronger, more developed recent works. Mr. Miller also offers advice for further progress that can be tracked and discussed in future writing and conversations.

Grade Yourself: Marking-Period Conferences

In Mr. Kim's twelfth grade AP literature class, he has implemented a nontraditional grading system. Instead of receiving overall marks on assignments, students are evaluated on a set of standards on writing-related skills. Whereas traditional grading marks are often based on completion or may not offer detailed evaluation on criteria, standards grading affords greater detail for instructors and students to see strengths and weaknesses on the same standards across assignments. In this context,

Mr. Kim asks students to make an argument about the grade they feel they deserve based on criteria agreed on by the class (see sample in textbox). In general, this includes performance across standards, completion of work, incorporation of feedback, and reflection on progress.

Grade Agreement (Based on Sarah Zerwin's Work)

MP	General Grading Criteria	Tracking Your Learning & Improvement	Completion of Work
A 90–100	• Engaged and reflective in your own learning and progress on goals. • Avoided assignments marked as late. • Close to 5.0 standard average: mid to high 90s. • +4.5 standard average: high 80s to low 90s. • Made sure you are keeping meaningful records of your learning toward the course goals. • Careful attention to feedback. • Potentially took part in extra activities, including Saturday sessions, field trips, or other "extra credit" opportunities.	Track your learning on goals and show definitive evidence of **meaningful and possibly significant growth or achievement in each standard and goal**.	**Do all the work**. No missing assignments.
B 80–89	• Show some engagement and reflection in your own learning and progress. • +4.5 standard average: 85–90s. • +4.0 standard average: approx. 80–85. • Learning standard scores are still strong but may not demonstrate mastery level consistently. • Could be more focused on keeping track of your learning. • Could be somewhat more attentive in attention to feedback.	Track your learning toward course goals and show some evidence of meaningful growth in each one.	Do the work, but maybe turn in one or two minor assignments late.
C 70–79	• Concerns about reflection and engagement in progress and learning. • +3.5 standard average: approx. 75–80. • +3.0 standard average: approx. 70–75. • Learning standard scores suggest room for improvement. • Possibly assignments turned in late. • Keep track of learning, but not very meaningfully. • Could be more attentive in attention to feedback.	Track your learning toward course goals with some evidence of growth, but there could be more.	Miss 2–3 minor assignments.

D 60–69	• Lack of work and lack of evidence. • Problems with attention to feedback. • 2.5 standard average or lower: get your act together; we should have a serious conversation about how to improve.	Track a few course goals; have little evidence of growth.	Missing work exceeds 2–3 assignments.
F	• Significant concerns about completion of work and attention to detail. • We should probably meet with parents or guidance counselor to help get you back on track.		Work not complete or didn't fulfill requirements.

Five-Point Standards Grade Mark Scale

5: Fully met the expectation of this standard

4: Approaching expectation of this standard

3: Needs additional work or revision to meet this standard; or may have inconsistency w/the standard

2: Not meeting expectation of this standard

1: Major problems/did not attempt (may want to see me for clarification & strategies on how to meet this standard)

Course Goals & Standards for AP Language

1. My thesis statements are clear and anchor my paper. (Argument and synthesis: take a clear stand; rhetorical analysis follows format and effectively articulates author's purpose.)
2. I use appropriate and convincing textual evidence to support my position.
3. I thoroughly explain evidence and make clear connections to my argument.
4. My arguments are sufficiently developed.
5. I can address a counterargument thoroughly and completely with an example from the opposing view and offer a substantial (re)assertion of my own position.
6. I can read critically and carefully: discerning author's tone, purpose, audience, and rhetorical strategies.
7. I can make clear connections between an author's use of language (rhetorical strategies, diction) and his or her purpose. ("In order to"!)
8. I can vary my sentence structures to make my writing more engaging and sophisticated.
9. I can improve my vocabulary, learning new words.
10. I have few spelling and grammar errors in my writing.
11. Multiple-choice progress.

> 12. I make regular contributions to class discussion, with specific references to the text to support responses.

Students come to the marking-period conference with a collection of work from the marking period, written responses (see questions), and a review of the gradebook with standards. In this sense, students are taking ownership of their own grade and are asserting what overall grade they feel they deserve. While this system is unorthodox and has its own set of limitations and drawbacks, the benefits are similar to those of conferencing with students. These conversations encourage students to be active participants in the construction of their grade, rather than passive recipients with less understanding and input.

After some trial and error, Mr. Kim honed some of the practices for these conferences. As mentioned in chapter 2, having a Google Doc with a grid for students' sign-up streamlined the process and avoided taking up class time for this (see chapter 2 for sample). Additionally, since these marking-period conferences took place over the course of the year, Mr. Kim created individual Google Docs for each student where he took notes on the conversation (see sample). These notes were helpful to reference for future conversations when discussing previous challenges and future goals. Due to time constraints, he used these practices in two of his five classes and focused on writing conferences in other sections. This allowed for spacing conferences out for different purposes in different classes, making time constraints more manageable.

Example of Marking-Period Conference Notes
    Student: Mina
    Date: November 20, 2018
    Standards Average: 3.27
    Number of Late/Missing Assignments: One late; one missing (Turnitin.com post)
    Strengths:

- Analyzing evidence
- Detailed answers to questions (but challenging when not clear understanding)
- Persuasive and convincing writer

Weaknesses:

- Inconsistent work—especially if reading was difficult
- Counterargument—working on not being too dismissive of opposing view
- GOAL: Please include two quotes/HW response or paragraph in essay.

- GOAL: In general, I think your writing just needs a little more careful attention; planning, including sufficient evidence; and reviewing before submission as much as possible.

Overall grade: 72; please ask me if I can clarify how to score higher in any given standard.

Mina is a high-performing student who has come in for a marking-period conference in March. Questions in the conference replicate the written responses students prepared in advance.

MR. KIM: So tell me about one of your successes or something you are proud of from this marking period [which is the first question Mina prepared].

MINA: The most notable thing I've done is the organization.

MR. KIM: Right. I see from our notes from our last conference, we talked about ways to reorganize your essay.

MINA: Yeah, I changed how I write my thesis. And then you see on this essay with the *The Beet Queen* your comment was that I organize my paragraphs to go chronologically through the text.

MR. KIM: Yes. I remember you had some really thoughtful analysis in that essay. Your discussion of Mary's character had some nice details. What is something you've struggled with this marking period?

MINA: I still find reading poetry difficult. Like what to do or write if I misunderstand a poem.

MR. KIM: What have you tried when that happens?

MINA: Sometimes I read the poem quietly aloud to myself. Like mouth the words to try and help me understand.

MR. KIM: A really good idea. I'm going to share that. Based on the grade agreement, what do you think your grade should be for the marking period?

MINA: Well, I completed all my work. My standards average is pretty high. I do well with the vocabulary standard, but I still need to work on my thesis statement standard. I think probably in the high 80s or so.

MR. KIM: I'd agree. I want to talk to all students before I finalize your grade, but it will likely be in that range.

✎ Teacher Reflection

This conference highlights some of the best reasons to have a summative reflective conference. Mina has reviewed her work over the course of the year and recognized how incorporating feedback improved her writing. Additionally, Mina has explained a strategy that provides an idea for a tool the rest of the class could use (reading poetry aloud). I can turn this around and share it with the class so that students with similar struggles can also utilize this strategy. —Mr. Kim

Finally, Mina is advocating for her own grade based on criteria, which ultimately gives her greater ownership in her grades and in her own learning. With few exceptions, students are reasonable in their grade self-evaluations. They may even be more critical in assessing their own work or grades than their instructors.

WHAT ARE OTHER STUDENTS DOING?

Reflective and portfolio conferences often take a broader view and wider scope in focus. Students will often be collecting, reviewing, and reflecting on a compilation of work. Therefore, students may need extra time to prepare. There could be incentives for students who go first in the conferences, and other students could be preparing during this time. If students are preparing simultaneously, they could try a "dress rehearsal" while other students are conferencing.

Dress Rehearsal

Students understandably are often nervous to present works in conferences, especially if it is in a panel format as portfolio conferences sometimes are. Whatever the potential format of a conference, a trial run will result in better preparation, support more meaningful conversation, and ease the nerves of students. There are a few ways to do this.

Students could pair up to practice with one other person. Alternatively, there could be groups of three, with one student practicing, one student playing the role of the teacher, and a third student taking notes to offer feedback after the conversation.

Another alternative is to have students record themselves at home as if they are in a conference on Flipgrid or an uploaded video to Google Classroom. With headphones in class, students could view one or two of their peers' videos, taking notes and offering praise and constructive feedback. Students are often self-conscious recording themselves, so this option may take some buildup in culture and expectations to execute; however, if students see the benefits of a safer space to practice, they may be able to get over some of their shyness.

Recording themselves in a video for other students to view will understandably cause a self-conscious panic for some students. Lower the stakes. Make it extra credit to record yourself talking about something personal and insignificant. Or level the playing field by making your own recording like this. When students are ready for the full assignment, use a model of yourself or another student—complete with flaws—doing the assignment. Show it in class in a low-stakes setting. It could take some work for the shyer students to feel comfortable, but this format has the benefit of protecting class time with the same performative practice that could help students prepare (also see chapter 3 for tips on using Flipgrid).

Additionally, viewing other students' practice runs helps them reflect on their own preparation: how do they compare? Teachers could also be thoughtful about groups of students viewing videos, placing students in groups that are friends or work well together. Feedback could be given in the form of written notes, a paragraph, or a letter or using a rubric. Grading students' feedback to each other as a significant grade (even if graded fairly quickly) will further their buy-in for the practice and ensure that they use the time productively.

SUMMARY

Reflective conferences are beneficial because they

- Demonstrate progress over time
- Provide opportunity for reflective writing, a practice often neglected in a busy school year
- Help instructors hone instruction as outcomes of conversations with students

Portfolio conferences are beneficial because they

- Offer a sense of accomplishment by acknowledging a volume of work from a whole unit, term, or year
- Enhance students' own sense of identity as writers

Effective conferences at this stage

- Include a range of work over time
- Use both positive and negative trends to make future goals

Marking-period conferences are beneficial because they

- Give the student voice in establishing his or her own grade
- Provide greater student ownership for progress and learning
- Promote positive and collaborative classroom rapport

Students who benefit from this type of conference are

- Writers who value process over product (this conversation highlights the process)
- Discouraged students who may not initially recognize the progress they have made

- Writers who benefit from seeing the larger picture of smaller assignments and overall skills
- Skeptical students who are unsure of steps for the following year as writers and scholars

Part III

Reflection

SEVEN
Challenges, Time Constraints, and Next Steps

You made it this far. There are quite a few options to insert conferences into the secondary education classroom. Do not feel like you need conferences at every stage of writing in the first semester. Pick and choose what is most manageable. For you, that might mean one conference the first semester and a couple more the next semester, depending on how comfortable the students and you feel. Taking time to survey and reflect after a conference could provide insight on what would work better next time. Progress, not perfection, is the goal. —Anita and Amy

Teachers want to conference with students but are often overwhelmed by the time and organization it takes to execute in an effective manner. The stages of the writing process are conducive to conversations with different students with divergent skills at moments when they benefit most.

In truth, a conferring classroom requires planning and thoughtful grouping. Even more vital is taking the time to create a culture where conversations about planning, writing, and revising are welcome and dynamic. You do not need to wait for the beginning of the next school year to start the process. One assignment in one term could be where you start this year. And that is certainly enough.

CHALLENGE: HOW DO I SEE EVERY STUDENT FOR A CONFERENCE?

If the goal is to see every student for every writing assignment, then no secondary teacher who teaches alone in a classroom will accomplish the goal without using up valuable time for prep and lunch. Try to avoid giving up preps or personal time outside of school by strategically seeing different students across the writing process in class.

So how do you figure out which conference styles benefit which student? The suggestions in table 7.1 identify the stages of writing and which students could be spoken to at each juncture for the most impact. Also, the types of conferences and chapters are included.

CHALLENGE: WHICH CLASSES SHOULD I CONFERENCE WITH?

Any student can benefit from conferences at any stage, but table 7.2 suggests how you might focus your time and energy based on class type. Students can also voice their preference for when in the writing process they would like to conference through surveys.

CHALLENGE: WHAT IS THE REST OF THE CLASS DOING?

Chapter 1 discussed the importance of building buy-in and accountability for conferencing, especially for those students not in a conference. Reviewing these practices will help support any other classroom assignment. If students are not held accountable for the work they do when the teacher is conducting a conference, then the conference is just a much-interrupted conversation.

Student accountability is not achieved through busy work. Students will recognize busy work as throwaway, inconsequential, and an opportunity for off-task conversation. Have the students engage in critical, necessary tasks that have clear objectives and deadlines. At any time, tasks related to the next unit are inherently not busy work, but be sure to explain the purpose of the assignment and how it connects to the next unit. Even if an entire period is devoted to conferences, classroom management practice dictates that you start the class with the objectives of the day, spend some time in the middle of the period taking a walk about the room to check on student progress, and then end the class with a debrief on whether task and teacher expectations were met.

Finally, a class that is accustomed to group work and that is comfortable working within the workshop model is already acclimated to the concept of accountability.

Table 7.3 shares tasks that students can engage in that are related to writing while the teacher is conferring with other students.

CHALLENGE: HOW DO I FREE UP CLASS TIME?

Conferencing does not have to be an onerous task that eats up valuable instructional time. Seeing students in groups for related skills or similarly

Table 7.1. Who to see at what stage

Writing Stage	Which Students Benefit	Which Conference to Utilize
Brainstorming & Outlining (chapter 3)	• ELL students who may have misunderstood the text or task. • Writers who struggle to break big tasks down into more manageable chunks. • Writers who have trouble getting started, but often prevail after the initial hump. • Perfectionists afraid of making initial (or any) mistakes.	**Before We Climb Mount Everest:** Using Brief Responses to Determine Early Needs **Elevator Pitch:** Quick Conversation to Test Ideas **Commit to a Topic:** Narrowing the Focus of Research Papers **Online Discussion:** Using Technology to Share Initial Thoughts **Talk Me through It:** Classic Outline Conference **Think Outside the Classroom:** Video-Recording Outline Conference
Drafting (chapter 4)	• Students who struggle with longer writing tasks. • Students who want advice to "see if they're on the right track." • Students who need a little extra encouragement to persevere.	**Set the Stage:** Sloppy Collective Writing for Follow-up Drafting Conferences **Quick Talk:** Incremental Deadlines and Flash Conference **Peer Edit:** Critical Friend **Stay on Target:** Troubleshooting Conferences for Specific Challenges
Revision (chapter 5)	• Students who want specific commentary. • Writers who started but are unable to finish the first draft. • Students who need to verbalize concerns. • Students who want to workshop their writing. • Those who need help seeing the strengths in their writing.	**Let's Talk:** Student Identification of Conversation Focus **Tell Me:** Providing Silence for Expression **Peer-to-Peer in Rounds:** Encouraging Written Student Conversation **Stations Lesson and Small-Group Conferencing:** Seeing All the Students **Technology-Driven Alternative:** Audio Comments **Skills Conference:** Focusing on Substance with Common Language

Reflective: Portfolio or Marking Period (chapter 6)	• Writers who value product over process (this conversation highlights the process). • Discouraged students who may not initially recognize the progress they have made. • Writers who benefit from seeing the larger picture of smaller assignments and overall skills. • Skeptical students who are unsure of steps for the following year as writers and scholars.	**Postgame Analysis:** Reviewing the First Major Writing Assignment **The Collected Works:** Portfolio Conferences **Grade Yourself:** Marking-Period Conference

focused conversations are time savers. Video-recording may be done outside class by the student and accessed at any time by the instructor. Audio comments by the teacher free up class time but can also be listened to by students and acted on while the teacher is conducting conferences.

CHALLENGE: OTHER POSSIBLE OBSTACLES TO CONFERENCING

There are many reasons secondary teachers opt out of a classroom culture of conferring. Most of those reasons have workarounds. Chapter 3 focused on specific obstacles teachers face at the onset of this classroom culture shift. Table 7.5 addresses ongoing issues in the course of a school year.

CHALLENGE: HOW DO I ADDRESS THE ISSUE OF STUDENTS WHO DO NOT WANT TO CONFERENCE?

For some students, the culture shift to this type of classroom is too much of an unknown. This student might not want to talk about their writing, might not want to have actionable feedback, or might not want to have any deep conversation with you. Do not select this student as your first writer to speak to; instead, wait until later in the writing process or in the student queue.

Some of the fear may subside once other students have completed their conferences, acted upon the feedback, and did not suffer unduly. The first conversation might be awkward, and let it be as brief as the student would like it to be. It's okay if nothing significant is discussed or even next steps agreed on. Rather, focus, outside of the conference, on establishing a relationship.

Table 7.2. Conferences for types of classes

Class	Conference
General education	Drafting (chapter 4)
	Revision (chapter 5)
ENL/ELL	Brainstorming (chapter 3)
ICT	Brainstorming (chapter 3)
	Outlining (chapter 3)
	Drafting (chapter 4)
AP/Advanced	Revision (chapter 5)
	Reflective and Marking Period (chapter 6)

There might be a defiant student who believes that any conference, whether about writing or an end-of-term or marking-period conversation, is a waste of time. Why bother, they might think, if the teacher has all the control and is the final voice of authority when it comes to grade distribution?

A partial solution for this circumstance might be a question posed to the student. Why are we here? What are we trying to accomplish? What is something you want to tell me beyond this assignment in front of us? Allay some fears; every student has a voice, each student's opinion matters, and you are not going to make a one-sided list of demands. Keep the interactions short until the student is less defiant or passive.

Some students find it difficult to speak to a person in authority and would rather be the passive recipient of grades. Teachers need to force students to get comfortable with circumstances in which they must challenge and justify.

CHALLENGE: WHAT ARE MY NEXT STEPS?

Conferencing seems doable in a secondary classroom, but what are the next steps that will not be too overwhelming?

Your conferencing to-do list:

1. Consider, early in the year, assignments to build classroom culture to foster conferencing. The goal is to know the students in a personal way beyond what their prior year's scores and grades indicate (chap. 1).
2. Figure out how to get student buy-in for conferencing. How can you include student voice in protocol creation and agreed-upon expectations (chaps. 1 and 2)?
3. Organize how to track progress, how to set up the classroom, and how to use co-teachers. Decide on which types of assignments and

what technology the students not in conferences could complete and use.
4. Based on needs, determine which students to focus on when in the writing process. You do not need to see all students at all stages. Determine which students may be grouped together to save time.
5. Make realistic goals: decide how many classes, students, and assignments to focus on as you begin. It is acceptable initially just to have one assignment in a semester or year. It is a learning process that will yield dividends in later executions as you reflect and refine.
6. Be strategic: determine which classes, students, and assignments benefit most from conferencing. Perhaps try the new protocols with one class the first year. Maybe it is the best behaved, most independent class that is the guinea pig. Perhaps it will be your smallest class.
7. Reflect by building in time to review and revise protocols, procedures, and goals for conferencing.
8. Build community if possible. Find a colleague to try conferencing with so you build support and accountability; plan strategically with co-teachers to maximize time and feedback opportunities.
9. Always do what is most comfortable for you. Do not do ten-minute conferences with every student; sometimes the discussion is just a couple of minutes. Do what is manageable for your own students, space, and practices.
10. Do not be afraid to chuck it when one way does not work. Be ready to experiment, reflect, and revise. That might mean administering class surveys where students can be honest about how the conferences were conducted, what worked well, and what did not.

Table 7.3. What other students are doing

Type of Conference	What Other Students Are Doing
Brainstorming and Outlining	• **Pitch It to a Peer** (chap. 3) • Searching for evidence • Continuing their own outline • Conferring on or evaluating peers' evidence or outlines • Beginning the writing task (for higher-skilled students) • Completing other short reading or writing tasks • Prepping for their conference (if applicable) • Google Forms survey asking students to evaluate their plan or asking questions about the assignment
Drafting	• **Critical Friend:** Peer Edit (chap. 4) • **Highlight and Index** (chap. 4) • Drafting in class

Challenges, Time Constraints, and Next Steps

	• Keep students on track with incremental deadlines (chap. 4)
Revision	• **Writing Groups:** Using Peers as a Source of Authentic Feedback (chap. 5)
	• **Love Letters:** Writing Friendly Feedback (chap. 5)
	• **Stations Lesson and Small-Group Conferencing:** Seeing All the Students (chap. 5)
	• Prep for conference such as **Tell Me** and **Let's Talk** (chap. 5)
	• **Peer-to-Peer in Rounds:** Encouraging Written Student Conversation (chap. 5)
	• Potentially start the revision process
Reflective	• **Dress Rehearsal:** Prepare/Practice for the Conference (chap. 6)
	• Timed writing, multiple choice, or independent reading
	• Completing other possible short reading or writing tasks
	• Video-recorded assignments submitted at the end of class

Table 7.4. Strategies to free up time

Strategies	• See students in small-group conferences during class time when they are collaborating—visit as many groups as possible; see stations lessons and small groups (chap. 5) and peer-to-peer in rounds (chap. 5).
	• Videoconferencing provides many of the same benefits and can be done outside of class; see discussion of Flipgrid (chap. 3).
	• Audio comments provide many of the same benefits and can be done outside of class (chap. 5).
	• If possible, foster buy-in from co-teacher(s) to split up students to conference with.

Table 7.5. Possible obstacles

Concern	Strategy
Classroom management	• Regroup and review culture-building practices (chap. 1).
	• Revisit individual benefits from conferencing, creating buy-in for focused classwork outside of conferences.
	• Enforce high expectations and accountability for work in class.
	• Potentially have shared Google Docs open so students are aware work can be checked at any time.
Space	• Engage in consistent protocols.
	• Be visible to class while still having personal conversations but on the periphery.
	• Have a designated space for student work storage.

	• If in a co-taught class, take advantage of outside space for conferencing.
Administrative concerns	• Alleviate potential concerns about nonconferencing students through use of task sheets, incremental deadlines (chaps. 2 and 4). • Demonstrate impact on instruction as a result of conferencing. • Highlight data and assessment gleaned through conferencing. • Emphasize clear objectives for students both in conference and in class.
Getting students to conference with each other	• Revisit the culture and benefits of conferencing. • Reflect on how conferencing has impacted writing. • Use Flipgrid for videoconferencing. • Use peer edit practices as segue or supplement peer conferencing. • Model or fishbowl a conference, highlighting expectations and building culture. • Consider how readers can also improve as writers through conferencing about peers' work.
Fostering buy-in for a reluctant co-teacher	• Model and watch a conference in a class they do not teach with you; discuss together afterward. • Encourage small, manageable commitments to conferences with assigned integrated co-teaching (ICT) or ELL students. • Consider broader groups after initial focus on ICT students. • Continue to have regular check-ins about students' progress as well as conferencing practices. • Highlight and share the academic data and personal information gleaned through conferencing.
What else to conference about	• Overall grades and progress • Emotional check-ins • Independent reading • Class reading • Formative assessments • Presentations, projects, speeches, and other performative tasks • Group productivity and dynamics for any assignment

CONCLUSION

Conversation is how people communicate, bond, and progress. There is some comfort in standing in front of a classroom and talking at the students. There is a sense of control when we execute a mini-lesson and send the students off to workshop or apply new skills. There is certainly pride when we walk around and see students on task.

Yet there is another feeling when we sit down together, make eye contact, and converse. We wish that feeling for anyone teaching in a secondary education English class. We hope for students who will advocate for themselves to their teachers and who will eventually provide critical feedback to other students as teachers step back.

In conversation, students reveal themselves as writers and individuals. Conferencing allows space for those revelations and opportunities for growth. For some, this might not come easily at first, but repetition and reflection are ingredients for later success. Both of us, Amy and Anita, cannot imagine a nonconferring classroom. We have tried and failed and will continue to do both as we hone our skills in forty-four-minute blocks of time. The students' outcomes are so worth the trials and errors.

You should start small; do what makes sense for your classrooms, spaces, and students. You do not need to see every student in every class at every point: make it manageable enough that you want to incorporate conferencing more often, want to reflect and later refine. We take on the challenging work of conferencing to give students more autonomy over their writing and ownership of their learning. It all starts with one conversation.

References

Anderson, C. (2000). *How's it going? A practical guide to conferring with student writers.* Portsmouth, NH: Heinemann.
Anderson, C. (2009). *Strategic writing conferences: Smart conversations that move young writers forward; Grades 3–6.* Portsmouth, NH: Heinemann.
Anderson, C. (2018). *A teacher's guide to writing conferences.* Portsmouth, NH: Heinemann.
Baxa, S. (2015). Enhancing students' understanding and revision of narrative writing through self-assessment and dialogue: A qualitative multi-case study. *Qualitative Report, 20*(10), 1682–1708.
Brookhart, S. M. (2008). *How to give effective feedback to your students.* Alexandria, VA: Association for Supervision and Curriculum Development.
Calkins, L. (1994). *The art of teaching writing* (new ed.). Portsmouth, NH: Heinemann.
Calkins, L., Hartman, A., & White, Z. (2005). *One to one: The art of conferring with young writers.* Portsmouth, NH: Heinemann.
Consalvo, A., & Maloch, B. (2015). Keeping the teacher at arm's length: Student resistance in writing conferences in two high school classrooms. *Journal of Classroom Interaction, 50*(2), 120–32.
Coppola, S. (2017). *Renew! Become a better—and more authentic—writing teacher.* Portland, ME: Stenhouse.
Delpit, L. D. (1988). The silenced dialogue: Power and pedagogy in educating other people's children. *Harvard Educational Review, 58*(3), 280–99.
Gallagher, K. (2015). *In the best interest of students: Staying true to what works in the ELA classroom.* Portland, ME: Stenhouse.
Gallagher, K., & Kittle, P. (2018). *180 days: Two teachers and the quest to engage and empower adolescents.* Portsmouth, NH: Heinemann.
Glasswell, K., Parr, J., & McNaughton, S. (2003). Conferencing with struggling writers. *Language Arts, 80*(4), 291–98.
Goldberg, G., & Serravallo, J. (2007). *Conferring with readers: Supporting each student's growth and independence.* Portsmouth, NH: Heinemann.
Graves, D. H. (1983). *Writing: Teachers and children at work.* Exeter, NH: Heinemann Educational Books.
Harford, M. (2008). Beginning with the students: Ownership through reflection and goal-setting. *English Journal, 98*(1), 61–65.
Hawkins, L. K. (2016). The power of purposeful talk in the primary-grade writing conference. *Language Arts, 94*(1), 8–21.
Murray, D. M. (2004). *A writer teaches writing* (2nd ed.). Boston: Thomson/Heinle.
National Writing Project. (2010). Research brief: Writing project professional development continues to yield gains in student writing achievement (no. 2). https://archive.nwp.org/cs/public/download/nwp_file/14004/FINAL_2010_Research_Brief.pdf?x-r=pcfile_d
Ray, K. W., & Laminack, L. L. (2001). *The writing workshop: Working through the hard parts (and they're all hard parts).* Urbana, IL: National Council of Teachers of English.
Tharp, R. G., & Gallimore, R. (1991). The instructional conversation: Teaching and learning in social activity. NCRCDSLL Research Report. https://escholarship.org/uc/item/5th0939d

About the Authors

Anita Abraham has been a high school English teacher in NYC public schools for 15 years. With Amy, she has presented at the National Council of Teachers of English and was a semi-finalist for the Big Apple Awards and recipient of the Fund for Teachers Fellowship. She lives on Long Island with her husband and three children.

Amy Matthusen has been a high school English teacher in NYC public schools for 17 years. She presents regularly at the National Council of Teachers of English and has been published in *English Journal*. She has received teaching awards from the Fund for Teachers, The New Teacher Project, and the NYC Teaching Fellows, and has worked as a coach for teachers with the National Math Science Initiative. She lives on Long Island with her husband and three kids.

www.ingramcontent.com/pod-product-compliance
Lightning Source LLC
Chambersburg PA
CBHW020749230426
43665CB00009B/551